THE UPPER ROOM.

YOUR PLACE TO MEET GOD

Sar...

L.

INTERDENOMINATIONAL
INTERNATIONAL
INTERRACIAL

77 EDITIONS
35 LANGUAGES

The Upper Room
January–April 2013
Edited by Susan Hibbins

The Upper Room © BRF 2013
The Bible Reading Fellowship
15 The Chambers, Vineyard, Abingdon OX14 3FE
Tel: 01865 319700; Fax: 01865 319701
Email: enquiries@brf.org.uk
Website: www.brf.org.uk
BRF is a Registered Charity

ISBN 978 0 85746 108 7

Acknowledgments

The New Revised Standard Version of the Bible, Anglicized Edition, copyright © 1989, 1995 by the Division of Christian Education of the National Council of the Churches of Christ in the USA. Used by permission. All rights reserved.

The Holy Bible, New International Version, copyright © 1973, 1978, 1984 by International Bible Society. Used by permission of Hodder & Stoughton Publishers, a member of the Hachette Livre UK Group. All rights reserved. 'NIV' is a registered trademark of International Bible Society. UK trademark number 1448790.

Extracts from the Authorised Version of the Bible (The King James Bible), the rights in which are vested in the Crown, are reproduced by permission of the Crown's Patentee, Cambridge University Press.

Scriptures quoted from the Good News Bible published by The Bible Societies/HarperCollins Publishers Ltd, UK © American Bible Society 1966, 1971, 1976, 1992, used by permission.

Scripture quotations from *The Message*. Copyright © by Eugene H. Peterson 1993, 1994, 1995. Used by permission of NavPress Publishing Group.

Scripture taken from the New American Standard Bible®, copyright © 1960, 1962, 1963, 1968, 1971, 1972, 1975, 1977, 1995 by The Lockman Foundation. Used by permission.

Extracts from CEB copyright © 2011 by Common English Bible.

Printed in the UK by HSW Print.

The Upper Room: how to use this book

The Upper Room is ideal in helping us spend a quiet time with God each day. Each daily entry is based on a passage of scripture, and is followed by a meditation and prayer. Each person who contributes a meditation to the magazine seeks to relate their experience of God in a way that will help those who use *The Upper Room* every day.

Here are some guidelines to help you make best use of *The Upper Room*:

1. Read the passage of Scripture. It is a good idea to read it more than once, in order to have a fuller understanding of what it is about and what you can learn from it.
2. Read the meditation. How does it relate to your own experience? Can you identify with what the writer has outlined from their own experience or understanding?
3. Pray the written prayer. Think about how you can use it to relate to people you know, or situations that need your prayers today.
4. Think about the contributor who has written the meditation. Some *Upper Room* users include this person in their prayers for the day.
5. Meditate on the 'Thought for the Day', the 'Link2Life' and the 'Prayer Focus', perhaps using them again as the focus for prayer or direction for action.

Why is it important to have a daily quiet time? Many people will agree that it is the best way of keeping in touch every day with the God who sustains us, and who sends us out to do his will and show his love to the people we encounter each day. Meeting with God in this way reassures us of his presence with us, helps us to discern his will for us and makes us part of his worldwide family of Christian people through our prayers.

I hope that you will be encouraged as you use the magazine regularly as part of your daily devotions, and that God will richly bless you as you read his word and seek to learn more about him.

Susan Hibbins
UK Editor

In Times of/For Help with . . .

Below is a list of entries in this copy of *The Upper Room* relating to situations or emotions with which we may need help:

Addiction: Mar 13; Apr 9

Anxiety/stress: Jan 8, 19, 21; Feb 11; Mar 8

Assurance: Jan 2; Feb 13; Mar 17, 31; Apr 25

Bible reading: Jan 1, 30; Mar 12; Apr 10

Celebration: Jan 10, 26; Mar 25; Apr 3, 28

Change: Jan 2, 25

Christian community: Jan 9; Feb 3, 22; Apr 23

Compassion: Jan 15, 17, 31

Creation: Jan 18, 29; Feb 12, 28; Apr 30

Death/grief: Feb 9; Mar 5, 21

Doubt: Jan 4, 27; Feb 19

Encouragement: Jan 10, 20; Feb 5, 22; Mar 23, 24

Evangelism: Jan 11

Failure: Jan 29

Family: Jan 5, 9; Feb 15; Mar 2, 4, 25, Apr 2

Fear: Jan 21, 29; Feb 11; Mar 8, 16; Apr 18

Financial concerns: Feb 2

Forgiveness: Mar 1; Apr 6, 13

Freedom: Jan 16; Feb 18

Friendship: Apr 23

Generosity/giving: Feb 2; Mar 27

God's goodness/love: Jan 3, 5, 24; Feb 5, 8, 12; Mar 29, 31; Apr 1, 2, 25

God's presence: Jan 5, 27; Feb 13, 28; Mar 6, 8; Apr 18, 20

God's provision: Apr 27

Gratitude: Feb 3, 23; Apr 7, 28

Growth: Mar 7; Apr 19

Guidance: Jan 13, 19; Mar 20

Healing/illness: Jan 4, 27; Feb, 14; Mar 10, 17; Apr 15, 20, 22

Hope: Jan 21; Feb 10, 13; Mar 13, 17, 21, 31

Hospitality: Jan 28; Feb 4; Mar 11, 22

Job issues: Apr 27

Judging/tolerance: Jan 26; Feb 27; 19, Apr 19

Lent: Feb 13, 20, 25

Living our faith: Jan 3, 23; Feb 1, 6, 7, 27; Mar 26; Apr 4, 17, 29

Materialism: Apr 29

Mission/outreach: Jan 11, 17; Apr 8, 11

New beginnings: Jan 2, 9, 29; Feb 22; Mar 5, 13; Apr 1, 9

Obedience: Jan 4, 13, 23; Feb 6, 10; Mar 2

Parenting: Jan 5; Mar 28; Apr 22

Peace/unrest: Jan 15

Prayer: Jan 4, 8; Feb 20; Mar18; Apr 24

Renewal: Jan 3, 9, 14; Mar 12, 21

Repentance: Mar 1; Apr 6, 13

Salvation: Feb 19, 25; Mar 5, 10, 30; Apr 14

Serving: Jan 15, 31; Feb 4; Mar 15; Apr 8, 11, 27

Speaking about faith: Mar 26; Apr 8, 9, 24

Social issues: Jan 10, 15, 17; Feb 27; Mar 11; Apr 7

Spiritual gifts: Jan 20; Feb 2, 4, 21

Spiritual practices: Jan 1, 3; Feb 7, 20; Mar 7, 9, 12, Apr 21

Stewardship: Mar 27

Tolerance: Mar 11, 22

Tragedy/loss: Jan 8, 21, 25; Feb 9

Trust: Jan 2, 7; Feb 14, 16, 26; Mar 20; Apr 5, 11

Getting Here from There

'To every thing there is a season, and a time to every purpose under the heaven' (Ecclesiastes 3:1, KJV).

Ash Wednesday falls on 13 February this year. In the space of only 50 days, we rush from the Christmas joy of birth and life to the solemn imposition of ashes and reminder of death. How in the world do we get from here to there?

I have always fought the temptation to leap directly from Christmas to Easter, stopping only for a quick pancake on Shrove Tuesday. I'm more comfortable celebrating the birth and then the rebirth of our Saviour than contemplating the sacrificial days in between.

But this year's swift transition reminds me that God calls us to both places. We are his beloved children in both light and dark times. Maybe it's too easy to connect to the Christ child, cradled in his mother's arms, or to the risen Christ, surrounded by elated disciples. It is harder to give thanks for ashes.

Where are you most comfortable? Are you more drawn to celebration or silence? As I anticipate this year's Lenten season, I plan to challenge myself to reflect daily on the richness of the journey, as well as on the destination.

This year I will seek to step back and honour each day that passes. As we move quickly from one season to the next, these words remind us that our connection to God is constant. We are beloved children in darkness and in light, and in all the seasons in between.

Sarah Wilke
Publisher

The Editor writes...

I had an appointment in the city across lunchtime. I managed to find a space in the busy car park and started to walk towards the city centre. The streets were crowded with shoppers, office workers on their lunch breaks and, as it was the school holidays, mothers and children.

It was the noise that struck me first. Even before I reached the main shopping area I was aware of a great cacophony of sound. Hurrying feet; music from a fairground ride in a city square; delighted squeals of soaking children as they ran through a fountain, pursued by the shouts of their exasperated mothers; a group of teenage boys loudly sharing a joke. Church bells struck the hour. As a background theme was the roar of the traffic as it streamed constantly through the streets, and car horns commented loudly on any delay. Motorbikes buzzed around the queues like bees among flowers.

Then suddenly I heard it: a solitary piper playing the hymn tune 'Amazing Grace'. The haunting melody rose clear and true above all the other sounds around me.

I thought of how our lives can sometimes feel like a noisy city street, full of noise, confusion and too much busyness. We can feel bewildered by life's fast pace, finding ourselves with too much to do, hurrying from one commitment to another, becoming tired and harassed. Change comes upon us suddenly, when we least expect it, and causes us to have to move in a direction with which we feel uncomfortable and even afraid. People's attitudes or actions disappoint us, and we feel let down, sometimes impatient or angry. We feel our energy and resolve disappearing.

And then suddenly, we are aware of God's presence with us. A helpful word from a friend that we are on the right track, a gesture of comfort from a loved one, a remembrance of God's promises to us in the words of scripture or in a time of prayer or worship—all of these can reassure us that no matter how busy or noisy life becomes, God will be with us at every turn, in our busiest day, or our darkest night.

Susan Hibbins
Editor of the UK edition

PS: The Bible readings are selected with great care, and we urge you to include the suggested reading in your devotional time.

New Year's Resolution

Read Psalm 119:1–8
Blessed are they that keep [the Lord's] testimonies, and that seek him with the whole heart.
Psalm 119:2 (KJV)

I recently visited friends in South Carolina for Christmas. While I was there, the pastor of the church they attended asked me to read I Corinthians 13 in worship. Since I am blind, I read in Braille, moving carefully and deliberately through the apostle Paul's words about love.

After the service, the pastor said the way I read touched him deeply. Too often, we rush through Bible reading and do not take the time to meditate on what God wants to say to us through the words of scripture. The writer of Psalm 119 held a high view of God's word and righteousness, as the entire psalm shows clearly.

How much do we cherish this gift from the Lord, God's message to people everywhere? This reflection prompted me to resolve for the new year to study God's word more diligently so that I grow in my understanding and become more 'diligent and consistent in living what I believe'.

This year, as a New Year's resolution, I am determined to take more seriously what the Lord shows me in the pages of the Bible. Studying God's word moves us toward spiritual maturity. The Bible offers guidance for every day of our lives.

Prayer: *Dear Lord, help us this new year and every year to read and study your word more and to spend more time with you. Amen*

Thought for the day: The Bible is God's letter of love to us all.

Link2Life: *Resolve to study the Bible each day this year.*

Roger Brannon (Florida, US)

Being at Home

Read Jeremiah 29:1–7

Jesus answered, 'Whoever loves me will keep my word. My Father will love them, and we will come to them and make our home with them.'
John 14:23 (CEB)

My wife and I have moved to a new house in a new city. All that had become familiar over the last 20 years is gone. The comfort of our family home, my garden in its different seasons, the thoughts triggered by driving down our street, the familiar smell of my favourite café—all are gone.

Everything is new: a new house, new streets, new landscapes, new shops, new people. Since we moved I have realised how familiar places can define us. Where we are in the world gives us a sense of who we are. Familiar places prompt memories, influence our attitudes and ground us.

However, I find that who I am is much more than the places I have lived and the roles I have played. Our identity is more about being in Christ than about being in a place. Yes, letting go of all that had been warmly familiar was hard, but God offered rich assurances before we moved. When friends at our goodbye gathering were praying, they sang a song that included the line, 'and I will give you a home'. I felt God smiling, saying, 'Look to me.'

God is good, and he has provided a home for us. The more I look to him, the more I can feel at home here. I belong to God before I belong to a place, so I can go anywhere and be at home.

Prayer: *Loving God, beyond familiar sights, sounds and smells, you are our true home. Let us dwell fully in you, now and forever. Amen*

Thought for the day: Living with God, we are always at home.

John Franklin (Otago, New Zealand)

First Love

Read Revelation 2:1–7
Let them give thanks to the Lord for his unfailing love.
Psalm 107:15 (NIV)

Once a week or so, my husband and I go on a date. Though we've been married over 30 years, we still find that a quiet meal or a walk along the river gives us the time we need to reconnect.

Something similar is true in my relationship with God. If I don't spend regular time with God, our relationship could grow cold. This is what happened to members of the church at Ephesus. In Revelation 2:4–5, Jesus says to them, 'Yet I hold this against you: You have forsaken your first love. Remember the height from which you have fallen! Repent and do the things you did at first.' When my husband and I haven't had enough time together, we find that doing what we did at first—going on a date—helps to rekindle our love.

When I first came to believe in God, I remember feeling delightfully overwhelmed by love. I was full of love for God and for the people around me, and I knew that because of God's love for me I could endure anything that came at me. God continually calls us back to our first love, to his unfailing love.

Prayer: *Dear Lord, help us make time with you a part of every day and to share your love with the people near to us. Amen*

Thought for the day: What rekindles my love for God?

Alice Benavides (Oklahoma, US)

Just Pray

Read 1 Kings 17:17–23
Pray without ceasing.
1 Thessalonians 5:17 (NRSV)

Mary was very ill, and her condition seemed hopeless. Suffering from tuberculosis, she had become frail; almost everyone felt she was near death. Even her mother had called family members to visit Mary before she died. When we went to pray for her, my faith was shaken. Even as we prayed, I didn't believe her situation could change; I thought we would be called that same night to be informed of her death.

One month later, Mary was still alive—no better, but no worse. At church one morning I noticed Mary's mother crying. I was touched and began to ask God what to do. I felt the Holy Spirit prompting me to visit Mary again to pray for her. I hesitated because her situation seemed hopeless; everybody knew she was dying. But God said in my heart, 'Just do it.' So I obeyed. I went to Mary's house after the service and prayed, even though I didn't hold out any hope. I 'just did it'.

Two months later, I heard a knock at my door. When I opened it, Mary walked in. I didn't know it was she until she introduced herself. Mary is evidence of God's power to heal.

When you feel God's prompting to pray, do it.

Prayer: *God of miracles, open our eyes to see your works, even in situations that seem impossible to us. Amen*

Thought for the day: When God calls you to do something, just do it.

Joseph Thomson Alum (Nairobi, Kenya)

On God's Palms

Read Psalm 31:14–24

Can a mother forget the baby at her breast and have no compassion on the child she has borne? Though she may forget, I will not forget you! See, I have engraved you on the palms of my hands.
Isaiah 49:15–16 (NIV)

My sister always seemed to be talking about her children—what they did when they got up, how they were doing in school, what little things they enjoyed. Everything about the children thrilled my sister, and I was pleased to share in her experiences.

I began thinking about how God delights in seeing us each day. He loves us even when we make mistakes. The Bible even says that we are engraved on the palms of his hands. Just as my sister carries pictures of her daughters in her purse, shows them to her friends and tells stories about them, our names are carried every day on the palms of God's hands. He does not forget us. God never will forget us.

Prayer: *Thank you, God, that we are important to you. Thank you for remembering us by name every day. As Jesus taught us, we pray, 'Our Father which art in heaven, Hallowed be thy name. Thy kingdom come. Thy will be done in earth, as it is in heaven. Give us this day our daily bread. And forgive us our debts, as we forgive our debtors. And lead us not into temptation, but deliver us from evil: For thine is the kingdom, and the power, and the glory, for ever.'* Amen*

Thought for the day: My name is engraved on the palms of God's hands.

Link2Life: *Speak to someone about God's love today.*

Marlene Brooker (Essex, England)

Puzzle Pieces

Read Matthew 1:18–25
All this took place to fulfil what had been spoken by the Lord through the prophet.
Matthew 1:22 (NRSV)

Jigsaw puzzles are challenging and fun. As piece by piece is fitted with others, a picture emerges. In a spiritual sense, we can see our lives as a meaningful picture slowly coming together, or we may see our lives as a hopeless jumble of puzzle pieces with colours and shapes that have no discernible pattern. The way we see our lives depends in part on our understanding of how God acts in human history.

Matthew's account of Christ's birth cites an Old Testament reference to fit the birth of Jesus into God's larger picture. Matthew wrote, 'All this took place to fulfil what had been spoken by the Lord.' Matthew's emphasis on the fulfilment of prophecy encourages us because it shows that God works through human history. We see God working through Jesus, and as we put our trust in Christ, we see our own lives fitting into what God is doing.

Day by day we can discover how new pieces fit into the puzzle. And a picture emerges—sometimes very slowly—and we can begin to see what God is doing.

Prayer: *Good and gracious God, bless us with faith to trust you day by day with each piece of our lives. In Jesus' name we pray. Amen*

Thought for the day: How can I fit into what God is doing today?

William H. Smith (Virginia, US)

Our Perspective

Read 1 Corinthians 13:8–12

Now we see but a poor reflection as in a mirror; then we shall see face to face.
1 Corinthians 13:12 (NIV)

Recently, I retired from my career of more than 30 years as a research scientist. Using an array of microscopes from simple to complex, I spent my days searching out underlying properties of a material or process that could affect product performance. However, I was aware that sometimes my interpretation might be imperfect.

The micro-world is composed of even smaller elements created by God, so small that even the most powerful microscope cannot reveal them. Our earthly view, as Paul wrote, is but 'a poor reflection as in a mirror'. Only God is able to see the building blocks that form us and influence our human interactions.

As a problem solver, I can be as efficient as possible with my microscopes and still fail to uncover that one key finding that would illuminate the problem. Outside of work, I face the same dilemma with inexplicable situations or behaviour. I remind myself that only God knows the fundamental elements that make up our existence. Our difficulty in understanding a situation often reflects the limits of our earthly perspective. We'll never be able to understand fully, but we can place our trust in the God who does.

Prayer: *O God, forgive us when our limited vision causes us to apply simple labels to complex matters, for only you in your wisdom fully know us. Amen*

Thought for the day: At least Someone knows what's going on.

David R. Stadden (Pennsylvania, US)

Floods

Read Psalm 143:1–11

Cast all your anxiety on him, because he cares for you.
1 Peter 5:7 (NRSV)

My son was affected by the flooding that has devastated more than half of Queensland, Australia. Lives were lost and farms destroyed. Just two weeks after the flooding, Cyclone Yassi wrought havoc in our state, wiping out towns, island resorts, and farming communities. I've struggled emotionally; I'm feeling fragmented. My emotions swing between high and low. As I try to concentrate on one situation, something else demands my attention.

The psalmists wrote about their fragmented lives. They poured out their needs to God in times of trouble, calling on God in the morning, at noon and in the evening. I've done just that and God has provided me with the spiritual help to get through the nights of restlessness to face each new day. I know from past experience that God walks with me through these troubles. Christian friends communicate with me, pray for me and encourage me. Even when it is hard to pray, I can read prayers that accurately describe my current situation. I believe that in casting my cares on the Lord I will find that God will sustain me and not let me fall. I will trust in the Lord.

Prayer: *In times of trouble, God, help us to cast our cares on you and find peace. Amen*

Thought for the day: We can always tell God honestly, exactly, what we feel.

Cora Williams (Queensland, Australia)

Name Change

Read Revelation 21:1–7

The nations shall see your vindication, and all the kings your glory; and you shall be called by a new name that the mouth of the Lord will give.
Isaiah 62:2 (NRSV)

One night as I was getting ready to start our youth-group meeting, one of the high-school boys came in with a grin spread wide across his face. 'Guess what?' he beamed. 'My name is not Chris Jackson anymore. It's Chris Farrow! My stepdad adopted me!' Chris' relationship to his stepdad had changed, and that change was shown by Chris' changing his last name.

In the Bible we read of various people receiving new names. God changed Abram's name to Abraham. God also changed Sarai to Sarah, Jacob to Israel, and Saul to Paul. All of these people experienced a dramatic change in their relationship with God, and their changed names reflected that experience.

Jesus will also change each of us. In fact, he already knows what he's going to call us. He knows everything about each of us. Inside and out, good things and bad things, just plain strange things— Jesus knows us, loves us, and has the perfect name picked out for us. Our name Christian shows that we have been changed, that we have been transformed by God's grace.

Prayer: *Dear Lord Jesus, thank you for your life-changing love for us. Help us always to seek deeper relationship with you. Amen*

Thought for the day: How are you living up to our family name: Christian?

Link2Life: *Think of ways you can help with youth work at your church.*

Stephen R. Wilson (Ohio, US)

Whose Image?

Read Genesis 1:26–28

God said, 'Let us make humankind in our image, according to our likeness.'

Genesis 1:26 (NRSV)

In ancient times, kings would put their image on coins and statues throughout their kingdoms so that people would recognise the king. Genesis is saying that, just as a king would place images of himself so people recognised who was their ruler, so God's image in human beings can help our world identify him as its true ruler.

Being created in the image of God gives us worth beyond our actions or achievements. We are God's creation from the beginning. Our destiny is to belong to God, and our mission is to live and share this truth.

This single statement from Genesis 1 quoted above can completely change our thinking about the dignity of humans and our equality with one another. Every human being, regardless of their station in life, is made in the divine image. Because God treats everyone as equal with no one valued over another, with no one left on the bottom, shouldn't you and I do the same? Each of us is made to experience life as God's image-bearer. This is why mistreatment of any person or group is serious. Justice can never be separated from the gospel of the kingdom of God.

Prayer: *Thank you, Lord, for creating us to reflect who you are. Help us to be faithful in doing so. Through Christ we pray. Amen*

Thought for the day: Each one of us uniquely brings God's image into the world.

James A. Brunner (Arizona, US)

In Time

Read 1 Corinthians 3:5–11

But how are they to call on one in whom they have not believed? And how are they to believe in one of whom they have never heard? And how are they to hear without someone to proclaim him?

Romans 10:14 (NRSV)

When I was young our family had holidays at our family's small farm-house. I saw farm workers plough the land and plant seed. They were followed by another set of workers who watered the crops. In time and with the careful tending by the workers, plants sprouted, then grew and matured to bear fruit. Then other workers harvested the fruit.

Jesus spoke of another kind of harvest, a harvest of souls. I was part of our church's evangelism team. We visited people in the community to tell them about Christ. Hearing the gospel did not persuade all of the people I visited. At times I felt sad, thinking I had not done my best. However, the important thing to remember is that those who were not persuaded at first may still come to follow Christ.

I realised that God's word is powerful. When God's word is proclaimed and shared, it is like a seed that germinates when the climate is right. Then sun, rain and caring hands contribute to its growth. We are God's farm-hands to proclaim the Good News—some planting, some nurturing, some seeing the harvest.

Prayer: *Creator God, thank you for all your messengers who proclaim the good news of your saving love. In Jesus' name we pray. Amen*

Thought for the day: How am I helping others come to know and follow Christ?

Minerva Perez (Santo Domingo, Dominican Republic)

The Greatest

Read 1 Corinthians 13:1–7

Now faith, hope, and love abide, these three; and the greatest of these is love.

1 Corinthians 13:13 (NRSV)

On my wedding day, our minister surprised me by beginning the ceremony by reading 1 Corinthians 13, which had not been included in the rehearsal the night before. Maybe the special occasion caused me to hear this text in a new way, for I remember coming away with new insight. I had always heard these words as overly sentimental and associated the word love with romance. I realised that nothing in the Corinthians passage suggests such an understanding. The Bible relates love to the self-giving behaviour of God.

As a recent graduate from theological college, I had studied faith extensively, especially its role in salvation and the Christian life. I had always thought faith was the premier power at work in the world. That day, though, I heard that the greatest of the three eternal attributes is love. What a wonderful way to begin a marriage! Without the wooing of God's love, I would never have come to faith in the first place. Without the love of my future spouse, I would never dream of making a lifelong commitment. And certainly, my love for our daughter these past 25 years has caused me to behave in ways I would not previously have imagined.

I've come to believe that love is the key to Christian living because when we love, the image of God is strongest in us.

Prayer: *Merciful God, help us always to remember the power of your love. Amen*

Thought for the day: Where and when have I been surprised by God's love?

Earl T. Dickerson (Kentucky, US)

'Is This Your Life?'

Read: Colossians 3:1–4

For me, to live is Christ.
Philippians 1:21 (NIV)

I was visiting a friend who I knew was a Christian. I had not known her long, but we had in common reading *The Upper Room*. She had spoken to me of the blessing she found in reading meditations from all over the world.

A copy of the magazine was lying on her table, and suddenly she laid her hand reverently across it and asked me directly, 'Is this your life?' We went on to share our experience of God's presence in our lives.

Later, I found myself thinking again about our conversation. Is God really my life, or just part of my life? How much time do I spend in his presence? Is God squeezed into a few minutes in the morning and again before I sleep? Do I ask for his guidance when I plan for the future? Some of my answers made me uncomfortable, and I felt humbled by my friend's question.

I want my life to be 'hidden with Christ in God' (Colossians 3:3), not for Christ to be a part of my life only when it is convenient for me. The next time I am asked, 'Is this your life?' I want to be able to reply with all my heart, 'For me, to live is Christ.'

Prayer: *Dear Lord Jesus, help us to give our life to you without holding back any part of it. Let us live in you and for you. Amen*

Thought for the day: How much of my life is God's?

Susan Hibbins (Lincolnshire, England)

What a Difference!

Read 2 Corinthians 6:1–2

There is salvation in no one else, for there is no other name under heaven given among mortals by which we must be saved.
Acts 4:12 (NRSV)

The darkest day of my life was 13 January 1982. After 35 years of self-centred living and countless poor decisions, I found myself standing in my barn on top of a bale of hay, with a rope around my neck. Just before I stepped into oblivion, I heard a still, small voice ask, 'What about your three sons?' In an instant, God used the thought of my children to show me that I could not turn my back on life. I removed the rope, stepped down, and decided to change my life. I knew, however, that I could not do it alone.

The next day, 14 January, found me in the science classroom of a teaching colleague who was a Christian. We talked, and I called on Jesus Christ to save me. That day, I became a new creation. In time, I attended a spiritual-renewal programme, and eventually began the process to enter the professional ministry. I retired from teaching, and on 2 July 2006, I gave my first sermon in the wonderful country church where I am privileged to serve as the minister.

No matter how badly we mishandle our lives, God does not forget us. His love and forgiveness are always available to give us a new start.

Prayer: *Loving God, help us to reach out to those who need to know that they are loved and that their lives matter. Amen*

Thought for the day: One conversation can transform a life.

Alfred A. Jaeger (New Jersey, US)

Creative Compassion

Read Matthew 5:38–48

Speak out for those who cannot speak, for the rights of all the destitute.
Proverbs 31:8 (NRSV)

Here in South Africa, we recently celebrated the 21st anniversary of Nelson Mandela's release from prison. I can still remember that day. I sat in front of the television watching history unfold. 'Tata Madiba', as he is affectionately known in South Africa, has played a major part in changing our nation. That someone can stand for peace and the inclusion of even his enemies in a new government after serving 27 years as a political prisoner is remarkable.

Jesus spoke about the power of non-violence. He called his followers to be creative and to point out the injustices in their communities. Jesus did not call us to retaliate. Retaliation only breeds more violence.

This passage from Matthew can lead us to meaningful ways to bring about justice and peace in our homes, in workplaces, in public settings. If we want to make a difference in the world, following Jesus' teachings will help us. We are not perfect, but the Spirit of God can make us instruments of grace, forgiveness, love and peace. Are we willing to let the Spirit work through us this day?

Prayer: *God of peace, work through us to make your ways known. Give us power to change lives. In the name of the Prince of Peace. Amen*

Thought for the day: God's love flowing through me to others can change the world.

Link2Life: *Learn about efforts for reconciliation around the world.*

Wessel Bentley (Gauteng, South Africa)

Phantom Pain

Read Psalm 103:8–13

He was pierced for our transgressions, he was crushed for our iniquities; the punishment that brought us peace was on him, and by his wounds we are healed.

Isaiah 53:5 (NIV)

One morning I heard a story on the radio about a man who had had his right arm amputated some time earlier. However, he still suffered something called 'phantom pain'. Though his physical arm was not there, the patient's brain still remembered the pain and sent out pain signals. The doctor retrained the patient by having him face a mirror and tell his brain that his right arm was gone. Over the course of therapy, the patient got better and eventually was free of the pain.

I can relate to that man's predicament. After I accepted Jesus as my personal Saviour, my sin and its penalty were gone. Jesus said on the cross, 'It is finished' (John 19:30). Yet after I became a Christian I did not always feel forgiven and free. I still suffered guilt and self-condemnation. This is a kind of phantom pain too.

This story on the radio challenged me to face myself in the mirror of God's word (see James 1:23). As 1 John 3:20 tells us, 'when our hearts condemn us… God is greater than our hearts'. As we come to believe that, we can be healed from phantom pain and guilt and be set free to walk in grace.

Prayer: *Almighty God, help us to remember that even when we feel guilty and worthless we can be set free by your grace. Amen*

Thought for the day: What vestiges of sin and guilt do I need to release into God's love?

Tracy Hsu Jensen (California, US)

A Forgotten People

Read Matthew 25:31–46

The king will say, '... for I was hungry and you gave me food, I was thirsty and you gave me something to drink, I was a stranger and you welcomed me.'

Matthew 25:35 (NRSV)

Our mission team was distributing clothes in a village about 350 miles from my home town in South India. At noon, I said to the local pastor, 'Let's have our lunch.' When I noticed that he and his wife had brought along very little food, I asked, 'Why didn't you bring lunch for yourselves?' They responded, 'People in this village usually eat only twice a day, morning and evening. They have no money for a noon meal. Since they have nothing to eat, how could we?'

We were stunned at these words from the pastor. We learned further that in addition to having only two meals a day, children from this village have to walk many miles to school. Those who are ill likewise have to walk to the hospital. To get drinking water, they must walk nine miles. They live with poor sanitation and no transport facilities.

I returned home thinking, How can they live without food, water, medical care, transport, schools? I believe that these painful and unjust conditions could and would change if we tuned our hearts to the heart of Jesus and found ways to bring his compassion and love to those in need.

Prayer: *O God, give each of us a heart like yours, full of compassion and love for the hurting people of our world. Help us find ways to make a difference for all your children in need. Amen*

Thought for the day: How do I meet the 'real needs' of those near me (see Titus 3:14)?

S. Rajan (Kerala, India)

God's Goodness

Read 2 Corinthians 4:6–12

O give thanks unto the Lord; for he is good; for his mercy endureth for ever.
Psalm 136:1 (KJV)

As I ride my horse along the paths that meander around the corn-fields, I realise how majestic and good God is. As my horse's hooves sound on the path, my thoughts are caught up in the moment and give thanks for the blessings he has given me. When I am alone with my horse in the countryside, I feel close to God. I am content and at peace. The cares and burdens of the day float away on the wind, and I am alone in God's company.

When I enjoy these good moments in life, I ask God to help me see the good even in the worst situations. I realise that life will not always be perfect and that I will encounter complications and trials along the way. I desire to be faithful and to praise God even when life hits me hard.

I have experienced God's goodness and mercy each day of my life. Reading his word and praying restores my soul and helps me to keep him first in my life. As my horse and I reach home, I again give thanks for all that God has done and ask him to strengthen my faith for the days to come.

Prayer: *Heavenly Lord, help us to see the good in bad situations and to recognise your presence every day of our lives. Amen*

Thought for the day: God blesses our lives with beauty and goodness.

Megan S. Feaser (Pennsylvania, US)

Pure Words

Read Psalm 32:6–11
Every word of God proves true.
Proverbs 30:5 (NRSV)

When I was a conscientious college student, my stomach knotted at the mention of the word 'test'. Despite hours of study, I worried that I'd studied the wrong facts. I feared forgetting what I'd memorised. Even after I had checked my work and given in the test paper, my elation was quickly replaced by self-doubt: had I done as well as I thought?

College tests have been replaced by tests with less clear-cut results. As a parent, I hope that I am teaching my children the skills they need to navigate life. Birthdays come and go, and I wonder how I will deal with the challenges of ageing. I won't know the results of these tests for many years.

But Proverbs 30:5 reassures us that the wisdom found in God's word survives life's tests. The Hebrew word in that verse translated 'proves true' is also translated 'is tested' (NASV) and 'is pure' (KJV). The image comes from the process of refining or purifying metal. Everything God says or does is for our good. The truth of scripture grows from and reflects God's love, which upholds and strengthens us in any test we face.

Prayer: *Lord, thank you for wisdom that we can stake our life on. Help us always to turn to you for guidance or comfort, trusting that you will answer. Amen*

Thought for the day: God's word is tested and proves true.

Shannon L. Hale (Missouri, US)

One of a Kind

Read 1 Corinthians 12:12–27
Each has a particular gift from God, one having one kind and another a different kind.
1 Corinthians 7:7 (NRSV)

A story once circulated about a devoted admirer of the famous Italian tenor Bejamino Gigli. The fan remarked that Gigli was indeed the second Caruso. Enrico Caruso was a great singer. As the story goes, Gigli responded, 'I am not a second Caruso. I am the first Gigli.'

I always smile when I recall this story, mainly because of Gigli's spontaneous and witty reaction. But his answer also reminds me of a deeper and important truth: God created each of us unique—that is, not aspiring or striving to be like someone else, not allowing anyone to prevent us from becoming who God wants us to be.

Of course strong and respected leaders deserve to be admired and followed. But the bigger challenge remains to discover, embrace and develop our own God-given talents. Because God has made each of us unique, each of us is indeed special—one of a kind.

Prayer: *Wise and loving God, thank you for the wonder of your creation. Thank you for making each one of us in your image. In Jesus' name we pray. Amen*

Thought for the day: Don't be the second anybody; be the first, only and wonderful you that God made.

Carel Anthonissen (Western Cape, South Africa)

Inescapable Grace

Read: Psalm 139:1–18
If God is for us, who is against us?
Romans 8: 31 (NRSV)

God is for us! I remember the first time I genuinely realised this truth. I was a recently abandoned young wife, living alone for the first time. Dejected, I sat in a sparsely furnished flat more than 1000 miles from family and friends—miserable, humiliated and very afraid.

Yet in the midst of all that fear, anxiety, shame and anger, I heard God saying through Psalm 139, 'Do you think I don't know? Do you think I don't care? Do you think I can't be trusted with your future? My grace is sufficient for you even in this' (see 2 Corinthians 12:9). And time proved that to be true. God and his people got me through that struggle and loss.

I think the apostle Paul heard a similar message on the road to Damascus (see Acts 9:1–19). Paul came to see and to say that 'in all things we are more than conquerors through him who loved us' (Romans 8:37). Nothing can separate us from God's all-powerful guidance, goodness and sustaining love.

Prayer: *Holy, glorious God, help us to seek your will and to listen for your voice. We pray to be yours in spirit and in truth. Amen*

Thought for the day: Nothing we can do deserves God's attention, but nothing about us escapes his care.

Jennifer L. Bryan (Kansas, US)

One Lost Sheep

Read Matthew 18:10–14

Rejoice with me, for I have found my sheep that was lost.
Luke 15:6 (NRSV)

I don't know about you, but when I think about the practical aspects of the parable of the lost sheep, I don't understand it. Why would the shepherd leave 99 sheep unprotected just to look for one that was lost? Wouldn't some of those 99 sheep wander off or even be attacked and killed by wild animals? Going after one sheep is simply not a practical solution to the problem. It seems to be a bad business decision.

But ultimately, I don't think this parable is intended as a practical solution to an everyday problem. I see it more as a description of the radical love that abounds in the kingdom of heaven. God loves us with such reckless abandon that he will ignore practicality in order to find us and bring us home. That's astounding love.

Prayer: *Dear God, we can't fully understand your radical, unmerited love for us. We can only kneel in thankful awe and humility. Help us to be like children in your presence, and grant us the faith to be disciples who fully love you in word and deed. Amen*

Thought for the day: How will I respond to God's radical love today?

Doug Ralls (Tennessee, US)

PRAYER FOCUS: THOSE WHO FEEL LOST

Play with Passion

Read 1 Corinthians 9:24–27

Since we are surrounded by such a great cloud of witnesses, let us throw off everything that hinders and the sin that so easily entangles, and let us run with perseverance the race marked out for us.
Hebrews 12:1 (NIV)

The two football teams were eagerly awaiting their match. Over the years they'd had a stormy history, and on this particular Saturday afternoon emotions were running high. Every player was fit and raring to go. The visitors played with skill and enthusiasm, and they won.

When fans were interviewed after the game, one man said, 'The visitors won because they played with passion.'

Passion makes a difference in many areas of life, including our faith journey. Are we passionate in serving God? Do we take every opportunity to share what we believe? Do we try to live Christ-like lives? How wonderful, if those who know us well can say of us that we live full of passion for Christ. I want to 'press on toward the goal' (see Philippians 3:14) of obedience to God, looking neither to the right nor to the left but fixing my eyes on Jesus (see Hebrews 12:2). What about you?

Prayer: *Heavenly Father, may we see clearly our one purpose in life: to serve and follow you as we pray, 'Father, hallowed be your name, your kingdom come. Give us each day our daily bread. Forgive us our sins, for we also forgive everyone who sins against us. And lead us not into temptation.'* Amen*

Thought for the day: How passionate am I in serving God?

Carol Purves (Cumbria, England)

Balancing Accounts

Read Titus 3:3–7

He saved us, not because of any works of righteousness that we had done, but according to his mercy, through the water of rebirth and renewal by the Holy Spirit.

Titus 3:5 (NRSV)

When I balance my cheque book, I confirm that my record matches my bank's record of my financial activity. I am good with numbers, and usually my account balances with the bank's.

This is not the way it works with spiritual accounts. The Bible proclaims that all people have sinned. Sin separates us from God. If we hope to be in relationship with God, something positive must balance the negative of our sin.

But nothing we can do is good enough to compensate for our sin. Only God has that power. He loves us enough that, through grace, Jesus' sacrifice outweighs our sin.

With my bank account, I do my part so that it balances. But when it comes to sin, only God is mighty enough to balance our account. He does this through grace. Praise the Lord!

Prayer: *Dear God, thank you for loving us so much that you are willing to forgive us our sin. Help us to love you in return. Amen*

Thought for the day: Only the love of God can cancel sin.

Gale A. Richards (Iowa, US)

Flash Freeze

Read Genesis 39:1–23
Yet I will rejoice in the Lord, I will be joyful in God my Saviour.
Habakkuk 3:18 (NIV)

This morning I awoke to a weather warning: 'Beware of flash freezing.' This alert is issued when the temperature drops suddenly, quickly changing a rainy day into an icy potential disaster. Something similar to this weather phenomenon happens to people, too. Life brings 'flash freezes'—sudden changes that leave us wondering where God is. In the Bible, we read about Joseph, a man who experienced many 'flash freezings'. Ice didn't make his journey treacherous, but the people around him did. When his brothers sold him into slavery (Genesis 37:12–28), Joseph's life changed in an instant.

Later he faced danger when Potiphar's beautiful wife's lies sent him to prison (Genesis 39:1–20). While Joseph seemed doomed to misery, 'the Lord was with him; he showed him kindness and granted him favour in the eyes of the prison warden' (Genesis 39:21). God knew Joseph's road was dangerous, yet he provided reminders of divine grace, kindness and favour.

When we face such sudden changes and losses, we may wonder where God is and be tempted to give up. But in such times we can remember that as with Joseph God is with us. He will show us kindness in the midst of tragedy and loss.

Prayer: *Dear Lord, show us kindness and grant us favour in the eyes of others. Teach us to trust you always. Amen*

Thought for the day: God steadies us when our way becomes treacherous.

Jason Mills (Ontario, Canada)

Other Sheep

Read John 10:14–16

Jesus said, 'I have other sheep that do not belong to this fold. I must bring them also, and they will listen to my voice. So there will be one flock, one shepherd.'
John 10:16 (NRSV)

When I was 17 years old, I participated in a foreign-exchange programme. For almost five months I went to school in Russia and lived with a Russian family. It was my first time away from my family for more than a couple of days. My well-meaning church back home sent several Bibles with me, certain that part of what I was called to do on that trip was to bear witness as a Christian.

However, after my arrival in Russia all those years ago, I soon discovered that God had been there long before I arrived. I experienced him through the people I met and loved and depended on during my visit. Although the way we worshipped and understood God differed, we all nonetheless experienced a loving relationship with our Creator.

When I recall this period in my life, I think about Jesus' words in John 10:16 about his sheep that belong to another fold. He doesn't say that the disciples must find the other sheep or that they will listen to anyone other than their shepherd. And he does not speak of them as being lost. Instead, Jesus said, 'There will be one flock, one shepherd.' Let us listen to the voice of our shepherd, Christ Jesus.

Prayer: *Holy One, help us to seek you and to not judge our ways of worship and belief above those of others. Amen*

Thought for the day: Human diversity is part of God's plan for our world.

Alissabeth Newton (Washington, US)

Look to the Hills

Read Psalm 121:1–8

I lift up my eyes to the hills—where does my help come from? My help comes from the Lord, the Maker of heaven and earth.
Psalm 121:1–2 (NIV)

When I moved to Middle Tennessee, I sorely missed the East Tennessee mountains where I grew up. Never before had I realised how comforting their presence was to me. I felt protected—almost enfolded—by them.

For this reason, I can relate to the scripture quoted above. It took a while for me to appreciate the beauty of the mountains, and likewise, it has taken me years to become aware of the beauty and comfort of God's presence. I've been through times of doubt in my faith journey, such as when my mother died and when I was diagnosed with a chronic disease; but like the mountains I love, God was always present.

When I get bogged down in the problems of daily life, I look at a picture of mountains that hangs in my office. It reminds me to lift my eyes. Even if these mountains are just in my imagination, seeing them reminds me that my help indeed comes from the Lord.

Prayer: *Dear God, thank you for your constant presence with us, even when we don't realise you are there. Help us always to trust in you. Amen*

Thought for the day: God is always present, watching over us.

Link2Life: *Telephone someone you know who is moving to a new area soon.*

Anne Leonard Trudel (Tennessee, US)

Hospitality

Read Genesis 18:1–15

Do not neglect to show hospitality to strangers, for by doing that some have entertained angels without knowing it.
Hebrews 13:2 (NRSV)

During my high-school years I worked in the garden of a wonderful woman who lived a life of much caring and kindness. Often after I had worked all afternoon in the hot sun, she would bring me a tall glass of lemonade. She also showered me with small gifts and homemade treats. Her grace-filled hospitality shaped my life.

The Bible is replete with examples of, and requests for, hospitality. We are commanded to show hospitality to the stranger in our land (Genesis 18:1–7), as well as to open our homes to those in need (see Romans 12:13; Isaiah 58:6–10; Hebrews 13:2). By doing so we may discover that God has drawn especially near to us.

Hospitality is at the centre of the gospel. The Bible tells us that God has come to us in Christ, received us as children, and given us all that we need. Our faith in God's love moves us to show this same hospitality to others.

Each day we can be thankful for the hospitable acts of others. And as a response to God's love coming to us through them, we can look for ways to show 'hospitality and welcome' to all we encounter.

Prayer: *Welcoming God, thank you for sustaining us with your love and giving us all that we need. Help us to open our hands and our hearts to others. Amen*

Thought for the day: Hospitality can express God's love.

Todd Outcalt (Indiana, US)

Becoming a Butterfly

Read Ephesians 2:1–10

So if anyone is in Christ, there is a new creation: everything old has passed away; see, everything has become new!
2 Corinthians 5:17 (NRSV)

Have you ever watched a butterfly working its way out of a cocoon? The process requires an agonising struggle.

Anyone who does not understand the purpose of the struggle might in sympathy snip the cocoon. This would make it easier for the butterfly to get out, but the butterfly would probably be under-developed and may never fly. The struggle is part of the process of developing strong wings.

For many years of my Christian life I felt like a butterfly trapped in a cocoon—a cocoon of secular values, philosophy and standards. Struggling through my feelings of inferiority, fear and failure was agonising and time-consuming. However, shortening this spiritual metamorphosis would have resulted in a weak, superficial Christian life.

I became a new creature when I accepted Christ as my personal Saviour. Slowly, like an emerging butterfly, I was freed. I found spiritual freedom in Christ.

Christ desires every one of his followers to live unencumbered by their old nature and to develop strong wings—to fly free as new creations in Christ.

Prayer: *Dear Lord, give us strength and courage to grow into spiritual freedom. Amen*

Thought for the day: Reaching the flight of freedom is worth the struggle it may take to get there.

Sandra Hastings (Rheinland-Pfalz, Germany)

In the Beginning

Read Genesis 1:1–5

The grace of the Lord Jesus be with all the saints. Amen.
Revelation 22:21 (NRSV)

I breathed a satisfied sigh as I closed the Bible. It had taken me three years, but I had read every word, working slowly to be sure I understood what I was reading. What a rich experience it had been! By going to the true source, I had learned a great deal about my own faith and about the experiences of those before me.

Throughout my reading, I was struck by how blessed we are to be the beloved children of God. It isn't something we deserve in any way but instead is the gift of a loving and gracious God who cares for us even when we sin. Time after time, as we read in the Old and New Testaments, we see people reject God; but still his love for them never wavers.

After finishing the Bible, I wondered where I would go next for my spiritual reading. There are, of course, many wonderful books that can help us grow in faith and in the knowledge of God. But at that particular moment in my life, the answer was simple: I opened to Genesis and began to read, 'In the beginning…'.

Prayer: *Loving God, help us to learn about you from the wisdom of the Bible. As we read, give us not just understanding but the will to embody your truth. Amen*

Thought for the day: As we grow in love for the Bible, we embody its truth in ever-deepening ways.

Link2Life: *Begin reading right through the Bible.*

Mary Van Keuren (New York, US)

By Word and Deed

Read Job 2:11–13

Rejoice with those who rejoice, weep with those who weep.
Romans 12:15 (NRSV)

I was deeply concerned about someone who is dear to me. The grey, cold day of constant rain made me feel even worse.

At work as I stood by the window and sobbed, one of my colleagues came up to me. He told me that everything would be OK. However, these words did not comfort me. In fact, they made me feel worse. A while later, another person came up to me. Seeing that I was suffering, he did not say anything but simply gave me a hug and stayed with me. This silent sympathy and empathy did far more for me than words.

He did what the apostle Paul urges us to do: 'weep with those who weep' (Romans 12:15). Today's reading, in which Job's friends mourned with him, reminded me that words of comfort can be important but that there is another kind of consolation—simply to be quiet together.

Prayer: *Dear Lord, thank you for the comfort you send us through our friends. Help us to be sensitive to others' pain and accompany them through hardship. Amen*

Thought for the day: Which should I choose today to show God's love and comfort: words or actions?

Irina Ivanova (Pskov, Russia)

In Life's Darkness

Read Matthew 5:14–16

People [do not] light a lamp and put it under a bowl. Instead they put it on its stand, and it gives light to everyone in the house.
Matthew 5:15 (NIV)

I was at the most crucial step in a delicate repair job when the lights suddenly went off. Total darkness! Fortunately, I found a small torch in my toolbox, and with its tiny beam I was able to complete the job.

The parallel of this experience with faith was obvious to me. I think we are all like that torch: small beams of light gleaming in life's darkness to show others the way to God. The Bible abounds with references to light in the context of our faith. In Matthew 5:14, Jesus refers to his disciples as 'the light of the world'. In the following verse, he encourages his followers to 'let your light shine before others, that they may see your good deeds and glorify your Father in heaven' (Matthew 5:16).

While the torch beams of our personal faith may not always be the brightest, or even the most reliable, nevertheless they can shine in the darkness. We can light the way for people to find a relationship with Christ. And it is crucial that we do so.

Prayer: *Dear Father, please help us to 'live and move and have our being' (see Acts 17:28) in your holy radiance, reflecting that light to others. Amen*

Thought for the day: How is your light shining?

Tuck Eudy (Florida, US)

From the Heart

Read Luke 20:45—21:4
Jesus said, 'This poor widow has put in more than all of them.'
Luke 21:3 (NRSV)

When I stopped working at a full-time job, I wondered how I could earn some extra money. I knew that God would lead me to a way I could use my talents, so I continued reading the Bible and devotional books regularly.

Each day after completing my housework, I began to write articles online. I received positive feedback for my articles, so I have continued to write, inspired by God.

From the small amount of money I received for my writing, I began to bring my tithe for an offering at Sunday worship. But I noticed that many people in my congregation were giving much more than I. I questioned myself, wondering if I were giving enough and feeling guilty that I was not giving more.

In the midst of this experience, I received an affirmation when God reminded me of the story from Luke 21 where Jesus commended the widow for giving her two copper coins. 'Truly I tell you,' said Jesus, 'this poor widow has put in more than all of them.'

Then I realised that our circumstances are all different. The amount of my tithe is not the important part; what is important is that I choose to give to God from what he has given me.

Prayer: *We find joy, O God, in giving to you. You have blessed us with gifts great and small. May we be faithful in using them for your glory. Amen*

Thought for the day: We give to God because he has given to us.

Arundhathi Enamela (Andhra Pradesh, India)

What Do These Stones Mean?

Read Joshua 4:1–7

These stones shall be to the Israelites a memorial forever.
Joshua 4:7 (NRSV)

When I officiate at weddings, I ask the married people attending to touch their wedding rings. When I touch my ring, I remember what happened 45 years ago when that ring was first placed on my finger. I also remember who I am because of the covenant I entered into that day. Mary Ann, my wife, and I pledged to be together as husband and wife for as long as we live.

The Bible tells us that remembering is important to our identity. When Joshua led the Israelites across the Jordan River into the promised land, he instructed them to make a pile of twelve stones that they would gather from the middle of the dried-up river. Twelve stones for the twelve tribes would remind generations to come of how God had brought the people of Israel into their land. The stones would also remind coming generations of who they were—the people of God. 'When your children ask in time to come, "What do these stones mean to you?" then you shall tell them…' (Joshua 4:6–7).

Reminders of what God has done in our lives are important to our faith. Let us remember and be thankful.

Prayer: *Call us to remember, dear Lord, what you have done and who we are because of your work in our lives. Amen*

Thought for the day: What helps you to remember how God has acted in your life?

H. Mark Abbott (Washington, US)

Kitchen Sacrifices

Read James 2:14–26

Do not forget to do good and to help one another, because these are the sacrifices that please God.

Hebrews 13:16 (GNB)

As I measured the flour and kneaded the bread dough, I thought of the people who would later enjoy this offering from my kitchen. A recent operation had prevented me from eating many foods, but I still loved to cook. My husband's colleagues and our extended family received most of what I baked.

The story of Martha helped me to view my baking as a ministry. She used her God-given talent of hospitality to show her joy at having Jesus in her home and having the chance to make him comfortable and welcome. Martha demonstrated her faith through her actions, as we are told to do in James 2.

As I reflected on Hebrews 13:16, I realised that I can express my faith and love through my 'kitchen sacrifices', by taking meals, soup or treats to the housebound, new mothers, neighbours or busy, working families. When I prepare these gifts with prayers for the recipients and deliver them with friendship and joy, I show others that God cares for them through the actions of his family on earth.

Prayer: *Heavenly Father, help us to share our faith with others by using the gifts and talents with which you have blessed us. Amen*

Thought for the day: How do my actions demonstrate my faith?

Susan R. Jones (Ohio, US)

God's Amazing 'Yes'

Read 1 Corinthians 1:26–31

[God] chose us in Christ before the foundation of the world to be holy and blameless before him in love.
Ephesians 1:4 (NRSV)

Every day I stand in need of God's amazing 'Yes'. God does not look at me and say, 'Well, you have certainly messed up. You aren't the kind of Christian or the kind of employee, the kind of student, the kind of parent that I expected.' God is not indecisive about whether or not I am worthy of love. On the contrary, even in spite of my sinfulness, God says 'Yes' to my worth.

To fallen and sinful people, God continually says 'Yes'. He says 'Yes' to people that I have not met. We might shy away from a homeless person or a starving man in Haiti or a woman dying of AIDS in Uganda or a child who rummages through a landfill site searching for clothes. But to all of these and to all of us, God says 'Yes'. All of us are created in his image; each one of us is valued and cherished.

By receiving God in Jesus Christ, I am able to say 'Yes' to others and to myself. In the dark moments of life when I feel like damaged goods; when I feel I am no longer meeting my or God's standards and expectations; when I feel lost, lonely or rejected, I know without a doubt that 'Yes' is God's unwavering word to me. And it is the only answer.

Prayer: *Good and gracious God, thank you for your amazing love to us that accepts us as we are. Amen*

Thought for the day: Where do you hear God speaking words of affirmation in your life?

Gregg Bunn (Tennessee, US)

Enemies

Read Exodus 23:4–5 and Luke 6:27–36

Jesus said, 'But I say to you, love your enemies, bless them that curse you, do good to them who hate you, and pray for them which despitefully use you, and persecute you; that ye may be the children of your Father which is in heaven.'

Matthew 5:44 (KJV)

Loving our enemies is not just a New Testament command. Exodus gives practical instructions about how to treat our enemies. According to Exodus, one who sees that the donkey of an enemy has fallen under its load must help. If we see an enemy's ox or donkey wandering off, we must return it (Exodus 23:4–5). In other words, when we see a mishap involving an enemy's property, we are not to turn a blind eye and let it be. Nor are we allowed to gloat or rejoice at another's misfortune. We are asked to help even people who hate us.

Jesus echoes this in Matthew 5:44–45. If someone is an enemy, we love her. If he curses us, we bless him. If she hates us, we do only good to her. If he is going out of his way to hurt us, we respond by praying for him.

God wants us to respond with love, not to make relationships worse by retaliating but to make them better by giving the best of ourselves.

Prayer: *Dear Lord, forgive us for hating our enemies. Help me to love them and treat them with kindness. Amen*

Thought for the day: Have you prayed for something good to happen to your enemies today?

Derek Sum Wei Siang (Kuala Lumpur, Malaysia)

Mistaken for Jesus

Read Philippians 2:1–11

Your attitude should be the same as that of Christ Jesus.
Philippians 2:5 (NIV)

Doug, my four-year-old son, accompanied me to the Communion rail, where we knelt together and opened our hands, preparing to be served. The pastor broke a piece from the loaf and placed it in Doug's hands. When he broke the bread for me, crumbs from the loaf fell to the floor. 'You spilled it, Jesus,' Doug whispered to the pastor. 'I know,' he replied. And he picked it up and continued to serve the rest of us, as Christ had served the disciples.

After worship, I asked the pastor, 'Have you been called Jesus before?'

'Yes,' he replied, 'several times, by little ones.'

Being mistaken for Christ seems unlikely. Yet shouldn't we want to live as Jesus did, so that others see him in the way we treat one another? Our call is, as much as we are able, to be like him.

I profess to be a Christian, but I don't always behave as one. When I'm unloving or judgmental, I'm not living as the gospel teaches. Participating in worship and assisting with various church projects helps me behave and feel like a Christian. But away from church, it's more difficult.

I need reminders through daily scripture reading or other spiritual reading. Each day, I pray for my attitudes and behaviour to be more like Jesus. I want to be mistaken for Christ.

Prayer: *Merciful God, help us to remember what Christ taught us and to follow his example. Help us to love one another as you love us. Amen*

Thought for the day: In what ways can I reflect Christ each day?

Mary Beth Oostenbrug (Iowa, US)

Necessities

Read John 10:1–10
From his fullness we have all received, grace upon grace.
John 1:16 (NRSV)

In school I learned about the necessities that make life possible. Oxygen is one; we have to have air to breathe. Water is another. Three days is about the maximum we can survive without fluids. Food is another of life's necessities. Clothing and shelter complete the list. There is, however, one necessity that my school curriculum overlooked.

I have learned that God's grace is a necessity. God is the creator of all life. When we are born into this world, we are also born into his grace. Without it, we could not survive. His grace is in the air we breathe. It is in the water we drink. It's in the food we eat and it's even in the materials that make up our clothing and our shelter.

We as God's people respond well to this grace when we give thanks and live faith. Giving thanks and living life to the full are faithful responses to the gift of his grace.

Prayer: *Dear God of grace, thank you for the gift of life. Inspire and empower us to live fully each day, to your honour and glory. 'Our Father in heaven, hallowed be your name, your kingdom come, your will be done on earth as it is in heaven. Give us today our daily bread. Forgive us our debts, as we also have forgiven our debtors. And lead us not into temptation, but deliver us from the evil one.' * Amen*

Thought for the day: Every moment of every day, God's grace sustains us.

Wayne Smith (Georgia, US)

PRAYER FOCUS: THOSE WHO DO NOT RECOGNISE GOD'S GRACE
* Matthew 6:9–13 (NIV)

Out of the Pit

Read Psalm 40:1–17

I put all my hope in the Lord. He leaned down to me; he listened to my cry for help.
Psalm 40:1 (CEB)

The day started as a happy time in the company of friends. But within a few hours, it became a living nightmare. Lisa, my three-year-old daughter, drowned. I demanded that God help us. I prayed that he would wake her up and restore her health. When it became clear that this was not to be, I prayed again, asking God to give me the strength to rebuild my life. I had to trust him to help me cope.

Some months later, we were trying to return to some kind of living, doing whatever we could to get through each painful hour. In my despair, I cried out to God for help and felt that he was inspiring me to write about the emotions and turmoil churning in me. When I did that, my healing began.

Eventually I published a book about my loss and my journey through grief after the death of our daughter. God has given me deep faith and the desire to help other bereaved parents. He has brought me to a place in life where I am truly happy once more.

Prayer: *Dear Lord, help us to believe that you are with us even during the darkest times of our lives. In the name of Jesus we pray. Amen*

Thought for the day: God can bring good out of even tragedy and loss.

Link2Life: *Send a card of condolence to someone you know who has lost a loved one.*

Betty Madill (Aberdeenshire, Scotland)

A New Testament Church

Read 1 Corinthians 1:1–17

Paul wrote, 'I give thanks to my God always for you because of the grace of God that has been given you in Christ Jesus.'
1 Corinthians 1:4 (NRSV)

Occasionally I hear people say, 'I wish we could be more like the New Testament church.' I always think, 'We are a lot more like the New Testament church than you probably realise!' Take the church in Corinth as an example. According to Paul, its problems included cliques among members, pride, sexual immorality, civil lawsuits, disputes, gluttony and drunkenness, and division over spiritual gifts. Some members even denied the resurrection of the dead. This New Testament church was not one we should try to be like.

Sometimes, the more we are involved in the inner workings of a church, the more discouraged we become. We discover petty jealousies, members who are not always kind to one another, Sunday school teachers who do not live as they teach, and ministers who do not always live as they preach. We may be tempted to give up on the church or to fantasise about a golden age that never truly existed.

Our church problems today would not surprise the apostle Paul. Yet Paul believed in grace for the church, not just for individuals. He gave thanks to God for the churches, knowing that Christ was working through them and that the testimony of Christ had been strengthened in them. He could believe and say all of these things not because the churches were faithful but because God is faithful.

Prayer: *Gracious God, help us to be the church you are calling us to be. When we fall short, pour out your grace on us. Amen*

Thought for the day: We can believe in the Church because God does.

Michael A. Macdonald (North Carolina, US)

Free from Fear

Read Matthew 25:14–29

The one who had received the one talent also came forward, saying, 'Master, I knew that you were a harsh man… so I was afraid…'
Matthew 25:24–25 (NRSV)

I was brought up by parents who loved me very much but were often critical. So I became unwilling to try new things, afraid of making a mistake. The servant who received one talent in the parable of the talents depicted me perfectly.

One summer when I was an adult, we had a beautiful crop of tomatoes. I wanted to try them in a new recipe. But what if it didn't come out right? Even in matters as small as this, I found myself hesitating for fear of failure. I took a deep breath and prayed for courage. The casserole turned out quite well.

I thought about all the times God had called me to do something new but I held back. This small act of trying something that I had been afraid to try felt liberating. I decided that I would remember that day the next time I felt God encouraging me to do something I had never done before.

Later I decided to take an online course in spiritual direction. The last time I took an academic course, the internet did not exist. But God's loving presence surrounded me as I logged on to the system, set up my password and answered questions. I made some mistakes, but I learned that I don't have to be perfect; God just wants me to try. I also learned that God does not want me to live in fear.

Prayer: *Loving God, help us to know that you love us even when we make mistakes. Challenge us to keep growing in love for ourselves, our neighbours and you. In Christ's name. Amen*

Thought for the day: God wants to release us from our fears.

Dorcas Linger Conrad (West Virginia, US)

PRAYER FOCUS: THOSE AFRAID TO TRY SOMETHING NEW

A Tiny Speck

Read Psalm 8:1–9

When I look up at your skies, at what your fingers made—the moon and the stars that you set firmly in place—what are human beings that you think about them; what are human beings that you pay attention to them?

Psalm 8:3–4 (CEB)

When my granddaughter, Lucy, was two years old, we went for a walk to post a letter. On the way to the postbox, we saw the moon, a great, bright, white orb hanging in the black sky; and she was filled with wonder. Months later, she still talked about it. We adults take the moon for granted. We know it's there, we expect to see it on nights when the sky is clear, and sometimes we ponder that humans have stood on it.

Imagine the psalmist outside at night, centuries before street lights. Perhaps the writer of Psalm 8 sat on a hillside looking after a flock, lying back, keeping half an eye on the sheep while gazing at the heavens. Psalm 8 captures the wonder of the night sky that Lucy felt. The psalmist realises how tiny and insignificant we are compared to the magnitude of the sky.

Even as the psalm recognises how small we are, it acknowledges the worth God gives us. Human beings are the pinnacle of God's creation. We are special. Look at the moon, marvel at the stars, and be thankful for the value God puts on you.

Prayer: *Almighty God and heavenly Father, thank you for making us special to you. Amen*

Thought for the day: In the vastness of the universe, God holds each of us tenderly.

Link2Life: *On a clear night, study the stars and planets.*

Pam Pointer (Wiltshire, England)

PRAYER FOCUS: ASTRONOMERS AND PHYSICISTS

Remember God's Love

Read Jeremiah 30:1–10

The Lord said to Jeremiah, 'Write in a book all the words that I have spoken to you.'
Jeremiah 30:2 (NRSV)

This passage from Jeremiah reminds me how short our memories can be. Jeremiah speaks to the people in a time of upheaval on behalf of the Lord. But before giving Jeremiah the message, God tells the prophet, 'Write this down.' Surely the people would not forget these powerful words of hope coming to them at a time of such deep grief, fear and pain?

Yet in peace or prosperity, we can quickly forget the trials of the past. This forgetting is dangerous, however, because it allows us to think we're self-sufficient and in control of our lives. Sometimes even in despair and suffering we can forget as well—forget the hope and assurance from God that our present situation is not the end.

The season of Lent comes each year as a time to help us remember. We reflect on our God who in Christ knows what it is to suffer and who meets us in our suffering to offer us hope. Discipleship is about remembering—remembering that to follow God is to hear the cries of suffering and to offer hope that only God can bring, to remember that peace is not something we achieve on our own. May this Lent be such a time for each one of us.

Prayer: *Dear Lord God, help us this day to remember your presence with those who suffer and with those who are well. Amen*

Thought for the day: Remember God's love and be thankful.

Eric Burton-Krieger (Tennessee, US)

PRAYER FOCUS: THOSE WHO HAVE FORGOTTEN GOD'S LOVE

A New Thing

Read Isaiah 44:1–5

The Lord says, 'I am about to do a new thing; now it springs forth, do you not perceive it? I will make a way in the wilderness and rivers in the desert.'

Isaiah 43:19 (NRSV)

In the middle of a long, cold Canadian winter, I am eager for spring to arrive. I can hardly wait for the snow to disappear so I can begin digging in my flowerbeds. As the warm weather arrives, I start checking for signs of new life in the soil. Sure enough, green shoots begin poking through the hard ground.

Isaiah 43:19 reminds me of the new life of spring and of the new life that emerged from my wilderness journey. When I was diagnosed with breast cancer, I felt like I was wandering through a desert. The road ahead seemed like a long wilderness journey. I wondered if anything good could possibly come out of this dark and difficult time. But sure enough, God made a river flow through the desert. He poured water on my parched soil. New life emerged as I experienced his faithfulness to me.

When we place our trust in God's faithful care, we are open to the new things he is doing in our lives. We are eternally being made new in our body, mind and spirit.

Prayer: *Creator of life, thank you for the new things you are doing in each of us. Amen*

Thought for the day: God is doing new things even while we walk in a wilderness.

Sandi Marr (Ontario, Canada)

A Big House

Read John 14:1–2

Jesus said, 'By this everyone will know that you are my disciples, if you have love for one another.'
John 13:35 (NRSV)

Recently I attended a funeral at which I heard Jesus' familiar promise that in his Father's house there are many rooms (John 14:2). These are reassuring words, partly because, for me, a house involves a family—the family of God together for eternity. I love this picture of heaven, conjuring up thoughts of reunions and reminiscences. But something inside me says, 'Hold on! Together? For ever?'

While I know the Lord has commanded us to love one another (see John 13:34), some of the people I have met are not always easy to love. I am sure they say the same about me. But I still find hope in Jesus' words. 'Many rooms' does give the impression of one family. Families are not always in the same room and do not always get along, but they are still families.

Why wait for heaven? Now is the time to love one another as unique creations of the same Father who loves each of us. Now, when I meet people, I try to remember to say to myself, God loves this person—enough to want to have them home for eternity!

Prayer: *Dear Father, teach us so to love others that we appreciate their uniqueness and how much you love them. Amen*

Thought for the day: God loves each of us enough to spend eternity with us.

Colin Harbach (Cumbria, England)

No Breakfast?

Read Luke 12:22–31

For all these things do the nations of the world seek after: and your Father knoweth that ye have need of these things. But rather seek ye the kingdom of God; and all these things shall be added unto you.
Luke 12:30–31 (KJV)

We woke up late on the morning of a big event at our church. As we got ready, my wife and I decided to save time by picking up breakfast en route.

As the children were getting in the car, their faces looked sad. Finally, one of the younger children began crying. 'You didn't give us any breakfast,' our five-year-old said.

As my wife told her that we would be picking up breakfast on the way to church, I chimed in and asked, 'Have we ever failed to give you something to eat?'

'No,' she replied. Once she realised that we would not let her down, she dried her tears and went happily to church.

Her fear of going hungry and having her needs unmet reminded me of my walk with God. Many times I have been sad or afraid that he has not heard my prayers, seen my need or realised that I was hungry. Like our daughter, I too have cried out when I felt God had forgotten me.

I am learning to trust that God promises never to leave us or to forsake us. He is always working on our behalf whether we can see it or not.

Prayer: *Dear Lord, remind us that you are always with us. Teach us to trust you even when we cannot see you. Amen*

Thought for the day: Whether we can see it or not, God is at work.

Cassius Rhue (South Carolina, US)

PRAYER FOCUS: HUNGRY CHILDREN

Listen to God's Voice

Read 1 Samuel 3:1–10

The Lord came and stood there, calling as before, 'Samuel! Samuel!' And Samuel said, 'Speak, for your servant is listening.'
1 Samuel 3:10 (NRSV)

A crested finch lives in my neighbourhood. I hear him far more than I ever see him. Every day I look forward to hearing his distinct call. Surprisingly, I can usually recognise the finch's call despite the morning air being filled with the songs of other birds. Yet at other times I can barely hear the finch's song, or I miss it altogether because I am involved in another task.

Similarly to hearing the finch's song among those of the other birds, I must make the effort to hear God's voice. The Old Testament passage above shows us how Samuel learned to recognise God's voice and to listen for it. Our fast-paced world makes it easy to become caught up in our commitments. Perhaps all we hear are the calls of our jobs, our families and our finances. Where is God's voice among all these?

When I take the time to slow down and still myself, to listen to God in prayer and through scripture, I learn to recognise God's voice. He has been there all along. I just need to listen.

Prayer: *Dear heavenly Father, help us to recognise your voice and to listen for it as we move through our busy days. Amen*

Thought for the day: God can lead us if we will listen.

Link2Life: *Take time out today to listen to the birds' songs.*

June L. Kanaski (Arizona, US)

Living Water

Read John 7:37–39

Jesus said, 'And let the one who believes in me drink. As the scripture has said, "Out of the believer's heart shall flow rivers of living water."'
John 7:38 (NRSV)

Recently snow slammed the Atlanta area where I live and kept people indoors for several days. After about three days being stuck in the house, I became weary and bored. I tried to find activities to keep me busy, but to no avail. As I stared out of the window at the snow, I reminded myself that it would soon melt and turn into water.

As I dwelled on this thought, I saw that our lives are often like this. Over time our hearts become frozen. Jesus, however, promised that those who believe in him would have 'rivers of living water flowing from within them'. In other words, those who are led by the Spirit are those whose lives flow freely and unceasingly from a never-ending Source.

When the sun hits the snow, it begins to melt and flow out into the world. In a similar way, as the Spirit touches our heavy, frozen hearts, we are slowly transformed into people through whom love, grace and peace naturally flow out into the world.

Prayer: *Loving God, send your Spirit to free our hearts to serve your kingdom. Melt away our selfishness, and make us people of humble love. Amen*

Thought for the day: When we let God thaw our frozen hearts, love will flow more freely through us.

Britt Hester (Georgia, US)

PRAYER FOCUS: THOSE WITHOUT CLEAN DRINKING WATER

Our Security

Read Exodus 12:1–28

The blood shall be a sign for you on the houses where you live: when I see the blood, I will pass over you.
Exodus 12:13 (NRSV)

I accepted Christ as my Saviour in my early childhood. However, my life was filled with fear for many years. I believed that if I were in the act of sinning when Jesus came back, I would be lost. This lack of assurance deprived me of the joy of being a child of God.

One day as I was reading a passage from Exodus 12, the reason that Israel's first-borns were spared suddenly lit up for me. God told the people to take some of the slaughtered animal blood and put it on the doorframes of the houses. Then he added: 'When I see the blood, I will pass over you.' God did not say, 'Here lives Moses. He is a man of God. So I will pass over.' Or 'Here, Miriam is not good enough.' He did not decide according to the person inside the house. The blood on the doorpost caused the destroyer to pass over.

This was a reminder to me that Jesus shed his blood for us. 'In [Christ] we have redemption through his blood, the forgiveness of our trespasses, according to the riches of his grace that he lavished on us' (Ephesians 1:7). The blood of Christ shed for us by grace is the source of our security. When doubts arise about our worth or our salvation, we can trust Jesus' work and words and not our feelings.

Prayer: *Thank you, Christ Jesus, for taking our place and cleansing us of our sin. In your name we pray. Amen*

Thought for the day: Our salvation depends not on who we are but on what Christ did.

Ruth Nussbaumer (Alsace, France)

Called to Pray

Read James 5:13–16
The prayer of the righteous is powerful and effective.
James 5:16 (NRSV)

In a sermon near the beginning of Lent, our minister suggested that instead of giving something up for Lent we take something up—some healthy habit or a practice helpful to others. I decided to take up the habit of praying each time I heard an emergency siren.

My prayers vary in length, but they always include thanks to God for the emergency workers—their selflessness and expertise—and a request that the lifesaving equipment they use will work as it should. I pray that the workers may arrive safely and that the situation they are responding to may be resolved as efficiently and effectively as possible. I pray also for those receiving emergency help that they stay calm and realise how best to allow the rescue workers to help. I pray for healing and awareness in all who are involved that God is with them. Even though one emergency siren is one too many, God is with both the helpers and the ones being helped.

This was my Lenten practice. For believers, many ordinary situations can become calls to prayer if we are open to God.

Prayer: *Dear Lord, we are thankful for the path of prayer, by which we may come to you on behalf of our neighbours. Amen*

Thought for the day: What life-giving spiritual practice can I take up for Lent?

Laura A. Martinsen (Virginia, US)

Hidden Talents

Read Romans 12:3–8
There are different kinds of gifts, but the same Spirit.
1 Corinthians 12:4 (NIV)

As I watched the liturgical dancers, choir members and musicians during a church presentation, I was envious that I did not have similar talents. I wondered what talent I had that would create the joy and excitement I saw on the faces of the people around me. I started to check off on a mental list the talents I do not have: I do not dance. I do not have a voice that any choir director would welcome. I am not musically inclined in any way.

As my 'do not' and 'cannot' list grew, my self-esteem plunged. What talent had God given me? Discouraged, I closed my eyes and prayed. Romans 12:6 came to mind: 'We have different gifts, according to the grace given us.' In the fog of my doubt, I saw a glimmer of hope. God has given me the ability to listen patiently and to offer encouragement to those who come to me with their problems or concerns. I can also write; and that talent, combined with my eye for photography, allows me to create a variety of multi-media projects to entertain family and friends. I realised that no matter what our gifts, God loves each of us. His only request is that we use our talents wisely and fully.

Prayer: *Thank you, God, for the gifts you have given each of us. Help us to appreciate them and to value them as you do. Amen*

Thought for the day: What are my talents, and how can I use them to serve God?

Link2Life: *List four or five of your talents and alongside them, ways you might use them to serve God.*

Mary Berger (New Mexico, US)

God is With Us

Read Isaiah 41:13–16
Love your neighbour as yourself.
Matthew 22:39 (NIV)

My life was difficult. My husband made me feel worthless. He told me not to go to church because I was not worthy of Jesus' love. I began to believe him, and I stopped going to church.

A lovely woman from the church came to visit me. During our conversation, she advised me to talk to the minister about my situation. She asked: 'Neri, what was the first Bible verse you memorised?'

I responded, 'Love your neighbour as yourself.' It became clear to me that I did not love myself. I knew that changes had to be made in my life and in my children's lives.

Later I read the passage from Isaiah that is our reading today and found the courage to put an end to a marriage that had trapped me. My children and I moved to another city. I began to breathe the fresh air of new life.

Today, one of my sons is studying for the ministry and the other son is a member of a musical group that leads worship in our church services. I took a lay pastor's course and have had many opportunities to put into practice what I have learned. I give thanks to God for transforming my life, and I know I have his blessing.

Prayer: *Dear God, thank you for your transforming love that brings us out of the despair of weakness and gives us strength to overcome adversity. Amen*

Thought for the day: God offers us freedom from all that limits and oppresses us.

Neri R. Gattinoni (Chubut, Argentina)

I'm Thankful

Read Psalm 105:1–6

It is good to give thanks to the Lord.
Psalm 92:1 (NRSV)

Many people greet each other by saying, 'Hello. How are you?' I noticed that if I reply with the usual, 'Fine', few people seem to notice. So I began to respond, 'I'm thankful.'

My answer brings interesting responses. My neighbour called across our gardens, 'How are you?' When I replied, 'I'm thankful', he asked, 'Why? What happened?' He assumed that something had gone well in order to cause me to be thankful. Shop assistants often greet me with 'How are you?' My 'I'm thankful' causes them to look up and to respond, 'That's great', 'Wonderful', or 'That's terrific.' Some express appreciation for my positive answer and thank me. This week, the school principal said, 'I look forward to your saying, "I'm thankful" each day.' Some people ask, 'Why are you thankful?' and I have an opportunity to tell them about God's blessings in my life.

If we take a moment to reflect, we can all think of many reasons to thank the Lord. Psalm 92:1 says, 'It is good to give thanks to the Lord.' Expressing gratitude is good for us and can be a blessing to others.

Prayer: *O God, give us thankful hearts so that we may acknowledge and share your goodness. Amen*

Thought for the day: How are you?

John M. Drescher (Pennsylvania, US)

Glimpses of Heaven

Read John 15:5–14

Thy kingdom come, thy will be done…
Matthew 6:10 (KJV)

When I looked into the beautiful, innocent eyes of the child in front of me, I realised that I was a part of the world she was experiencing. It was in my hands to express for her what our world is like—the world she had been born into. I vowed to grant her glimpses of heaven because heaven is what I wish for her. When she looks at me, I want her to feel joy, peace and love. And I want this not just for her.

In many ways I offer glimpses of heaven on earth for people around me.

When we live out Jesus' commandment to love one another (see John 15:12), we can bring heaven to people living in hell on earth. By helping to meet people's needs and treating them with love and kindness, I can help to change our world into God's kingdom on earth.

Prayer: *Help us, dear God, to bring your kingdom on earth for the people we encounter by showing them the love that you have for us all. We pray as Jesus taught us, saying, 'Our Father which art in heaven, Hallowed be thy name. Thy kingdom come. Thy will be done, as in heaven, so in earth. Give us day by day our daily bread. And forgive us our sins; for we also forgive every one that is indebted to us. And lead us not into temptation; but deliver us from evil.'* Amen

Thought for the day: What kind of world does God want for our children?

Einar Ingvi Magnusson (Hofudborgarsvaedid, Iceland)

Falling Short

Read Romans 3:21–26
All have sinned and fall short of the glory of God.
Romans 3:23 (NRSV)

Lent, more than any time in the Church year, brings us face to face with sinfulness. Though it may be difficult for some of us to think of ourselves as sinners, Paul boldly said, 'All have sinned and fall short of the glory of God.' None of us is spared the taint of sin because all of us have asserted our will against God.

Sin has such a hold on us that we do not have the power to break out of it by our own actions or through our resolutions or decisions. Sin is always there before us, and it is vast and inescapable. We cannot run away from it or hide from it or deny it. If we compare ourselves to others, we may feel virtuous; but we are no better and no worse than our neighbours. However, another comparison is larger and more important.

During Lent, we compare ourselves not to our neighbours but to Christ and to what God wants for us. We sin each time we fail to love as Christ taught us. Lent helps us to see ourselves as sinners and Easter brings the good news that Christ redeems us from that sin.

Prayer: *O God, thank you for loving us enough to redeem us from our sin. In Jesus' name we pray. Amen*

Thought for the day: Christ bridges the gap between who we are and who God calls us to be.

Joe E. Pennel, Jr. (Tennessee, US)

PRAYER FOCUS: FOR FAITHFULNESS IN LENTEN PRACTICES

Out of the Ruts

Read Matthew 14:13–33

Peter answered [Jesus], 'Lord, if it is you, command me to come to you on the water.'
Matthew 14:28 (NRSV)

One winter storm with heavy snow and driving winds would barely end, it seemed, before the next storm blasted in, leaving us housebound and waiting for it to clear. Those who lived in towns might have enjoyed a brief respite from their usual routine, but here on the farm we either had to get the food to the livestock or the livestock to the food. Horses pastured a mile from the house didn't seem far away until I had to haul feed to them on a road made invisible by snow drifts. Luckily for me someone had ventured out before me and 'broken a trail' that left a narrow, slippery track of ruts.

As I was following those and praying, 'Lord, please keep me in the ruts', I realised that spiritually I really needed God to do the opposite for me. I was in a spiritual rut. I was unwilling to face new challenges. I had often asked the Lord not only to keep me safe in uncomfortable experiences, but to keep me out of uncomfortable experiences.

Ruts are a safe place in a blizzard, but in our spiritual life ruts can be hazardous to our relationship with Christ. The passage from Matthew 14 tells us that Peter trusted Jesus enough to get out of the boat during a storm. We too can trust God enough to get out of the ruts that keep us from living more faithfully and abundantly.

Prayer: *Dear Lord, help us to trust you more than we fear situations that may surround us. Help us to get out of our ruts. Amen*

Thought for the day: Anything we can easily do ourselves doesn't require faith.

Jean Bonin (Alberta, Canada)

God's People Too

Read Romans 15:1–7

Share with God's people who are in need. Practise hospitality... be willing to associate with people of low position.

Romans 12:13, 16 (NIV)

I understood the people's reactions to me—the glancing looks, keeping their distance in silence. Like others in the waiting room, I was there to see the cardiologist. (I had recently experienced a heart attack.) But my orange prison tracksuit, shackles, handcuffs and two armed guards didn't exactly help me to fit in. Then an elderly woman walked in, smiled and said, 'God bless. I hope you're doing well.'

I responded, 'I'm fine.' Suddenly my anxious feelings were replaced with calm. 'Thank you,' I added.

Afterwards in the van heading back to the prison, I thought how that one person looked beyond the outward signs of what most consider a second-class citizen and saw a person—a person who, though surely one of God's own people, was in many ways estranged from the human family. Maybe it was simply that she saw an opportunity to do good.

The apostle Paul reminds us that as Christians we are called to show consideration and care for others, particularly for those in need and 'of low position'. While such actions may not always come naturally, our special effort can make a significant and lasting impression on people's lives. It did for me.

Prayer: *Dear God, open our eyes to those around us who are in need. Help us to see them as you do and to care for them with your compassion. Amen*

Thought for the day: Who can I reach out to who doesn't fit in?

Charles P. Axe (Pennsylvania, US)

Under God's Wings

Read Psalm 91:1–16

He will cover you with his feathers, and under his wings you will find refuge; his faithfulness will be your shield and rampart.

Psalm 91:4 (NRSV)

One afternoon while doing the washing-up, I watched a mother robin in the holly bush just outside my window. When rain began, she gently settled herself over her young fledglings. The rain soon became a downpour; the robin stood up in her nest and spread her wings wide. She rocked back and forth a few times, stretching her wings to create an umbrella over the nest. The rains pounded harder, yet she did not move. I watched her in amazement as I continued cleaning my kitchen. My chores completed, I hesitated to leave the room. The robin was still standing with wings outstretched, protecting her young.

The beauty of this scene reminded me of Psalm 91:4 and the refuge we have under God's protective wings. Life's trials are sometimes only a drizzle, and other times a fiercely pounding storm. But regardless of the intensity of the storms, God will be faithful. Though we may not always see God's wings spread over us, we can rest assured that they are there to offer us comfort.

Prayer: *O God, like that strong and faithful robin, you spread your love over us in life's storms. May we rest secure and feel your comfort even in times when we may not sense your presence. Amen*

Thought for the day: No matter how severe life's storms may be, God's wings are stronger and more constant.

Elizabeth Ann Bussey (Ohio, US)

PRAYER FOCUS: SOMEONE ENDURING A STORM IN LIFE

Courage to Keep on Praying

He raised his hand in a prayer workshop I was leading. 'I've come here for only one reason,' he said. 'I want to know why I should continue to pray.' He went on to describe several experiences in his life when God seemed to have moved away and left no forwarding address. The room fell silent, but I could tell that he had spoken what many of us were thinking and feeling. No matter how much we profess our faith in prayer, and no matter how devoutly we seek to practise it, always the nagging question lurks just off centre-stage: 'What difference does prayer really make?'

Scott Peck became famous for the opening sentence of his book, *The Road Less Travelled*: 'Life is difficult.' Many of the meditations in this edition of *The Upper Room* relate to these difficulties. Somehow, prayer has to be part of this; otherwise it becomes an ivory-tower experience that leaves us in spiritual limbo. So how do we find the courage to keep on praying?

I've come to believe that the courage to pray begins and ends with God. But instantly, we realise that not 'any old god' will do. In fact, some concepts of God are downright negative and counterproductive to cultivating a life of prayer. Some views of God are toxic and debilitating. Years ago, I was walking with a pastor friend, and I asked him what he had found to be his number-one problem in working with people. Without hesitation he replied, 'The notion that God is mad at them.'

Without some way to break through this notion, prayer can seem like talking in the dark or fiddling while Rome burns. None of us will give ourselves over the long haul to an exercise in futility. I have found only one way to move from thinking of God as distant and unmoved, and that is by looking at Jesus. Instead of revealing a God who is aloof, Jesus 'moved into the neighbourhood' (as Eugene Peterson puts it in *The Message*, John 1:14). And when he did, he showed us the face of a God who loves and cares—who never turns away—who walks with us even through the valley of the shadow of death (Psalm 23:4, KJV). And he went on to say what we all need to hear if prayer is to be real and vital: 'Whoever has seen me has seen the Father' (John 14:9, NRSV).

Whatever else this means, it means that God is not reluctant to hear and respond to us when we pray. When prayers seem to go unanswered, we can say one thing for sure: God didn't turn away. Life in a fallen world creates reasons for unanswered prayer that we will never be able to understand or explain. We have no choice but to live with this deep mystery, and sometimes doing so is very painful. But Jesus is Emmanuel, which means 'God is with us.' E. Stanley Jones said it this way: 'Jesus puts a face on God.' We all face struggles, sometimes over large things and sometimes over small ones. But what we discover through the witness of Christ is that we never face them alone.

At this point, we move into a second element that can help us maintain the courage to keep on praying. We come to the Church—the body of Christ. Unfortunately, when we move from Christ to the Church, we move from clarity into a mixed message. Most of us can remember tough times when the community of faith has failed us. We may have experienced the absence of the Church or maybe even judgment from its teachings and its people. When we are mistreated by God's people, it's easy to feel mistreated by God as well. But we must not equate what humans do with what God does.

Nevertheless, we are called to love and care. In this regard, I think of the people who carried their paralysed friend to Jesus (Mark 2:1–12). This parable helps us in two ways to keep praying. First, we sometimes find ourselves the ones on the stretcher. We must then rely on others to carry us into Christ's presence. At times we simply cannot pray—but others can pray for us. And that is legitimate prayer. Second, sometimes we can be one of those who carry the stretcher. We can weave our lives into the lives of others and become intercessors. This is part of our call as disciples of Jesus and members of Christ's body (see 1 Corinthians 12). Sometimes we must ask others to pray for us; at other times, we can respond to needs by praying for others. In either case, this is what the Church is meant to be and do.

When I look at Christ as he is and at the Church as it is supposed to be, I find courage to keep on praying. When we think of prayer as conversation which includes both listening and speaking, we realise an amazing and powerful thing: sound travels in both darkness and light. We can pray in the dark. Quite a few meditations remind us of this. You may want to read again those for January 4 and 8; February 17 and 20; March 2, 5, 8, 13, 21 and 28; and April 4, 9, 11, 15, 18, 20, 21 and 29 as you prepare to reflect on the following questions:

Questions for Reflection

1. Is there a particular image of Christ that gives you comfort and hope when you face difficult times?

2. Can you recall a tough time in your life when another believer became Christ to you?

3. How have you sought to be Christ to others, especially as you cross paths with hurting people?

4. Besides Christ and the Church, what other ideas or images enable you to keep praying with faith and hope?

5. Is there something you're dealing with at the moment that you'd like to ask Christ to help you with? Whom can you ask to join you in praying about this?

6. Who do you know who is going through a particularly hard time? What will you pray for on their behalf? As you do, ask Christ to show you how to add actions to your words.

Steve Harper was born in Texas. He is an elder in the United Methodist Church, retired from the Florida Annual Conference. Over the years he has served as a youth minister, evangelist, pastor, professor, and seminary administrator. He is the author or co-author of more than 20 books, and a frequent speaker and teacher in local churches, conferences, workshops and retreats.

Who's Keeping Records?

Read Matthew 18:23–35

[Love] keeps no record of wrongs.

1 Corinthians 13:5 (NIV)

My husband is a careful record-keeper. He tracks our monthly expenses and his students' test results. He records the scores of his favourite football team year by year. Some records are important to keep; others are fun to keep. However, I'm glad there are some records that God doesn't keep at all. When we repent of our sins, God forgives us and removes our transgressions 'as far as the east is from the west' (Psalm 103:12).

I love to think that God has wiped my sin record clean, but sometimes I'm reluctant to do the same for others. It's easy for me to keep a mental list of grievances. I recall times that people have hurt me with unkind words or actions. I see their faces; I remember what they said. Am I a secret record-keeper? When God has blotted out my transgressions, why do I hold on to hurts done to me? By God's grace, I resolve to stop my record keeping and to forgive as Christ has forgiven me.

Prayer: *Gracious God, thank you for blotting out our sins. Give us grace to erase the record of wrongs done to us, as we pray, 'Forgive us our sins, for we also forgive everyone who sins against us' (Luke 11:4). Amen*

Thought for the day: Because God is willing to forgive me, I can and will forgive others.

Link2Life: *Start to keep a record of God's grace in your life.*

Marion Speicher Brown (Florida, US)

'Go!'

Read Exodus 14:8–15

The Lord said to Moses, 'Why do you cry out to me? Tell the Israelites to go forward.'
Exodus 14:15 (NRSV)

Dengue fever was becoming prevalent in our area, and my son's fever was increasing. Because we didn't have any money and most private doctors in the Philippines do not offer credit, I thought we should stay at home and pray for healing. However, my wife insisted that we take him to the doctor even with no money in our pockets. On the way, we stopped by the ATM machine to check our account balance. We were amazed to find that my salary had been deposited early.

The Israelites found themselves in a similarly difficult position (Exodus 14). While fleeing from Egypt the Israelites were caught between the pursuing Egyptians and the Red Sea. Moses believed in the deliverance of God and exhorted the people to take courage, be silent, do nothing and see the salvation of God (vv. 13–14). But God told Moses to stop talking and go forward (v. 15), and when they went forward in faith, the Lord delivered them.

Sometimes when we think we are waiting patiently for God, we have actually become paralysed by fear and insecurity. At those times, we can pray. Then we can follow my wife's example and God's instruction and move forward in faith.

Prayer: *Dear Lord, give us wisdom to discern whether we need to wait patiently or to step out of our comfort zone—in obedience and with purpose. Amen*

Thought for the day: Is this a time when God is saying, 'Get up and go'?

Marc Villa-Real (Antipolo City, Philippines)

Reaching Out

Read Isaiah 40:31
When the cares of my heart are many, your consolations cheer my soul.
Psalm 94:19 (NRSV)

Five years ago I had a breakdown. Stomach churning and trembling, I curled up on the sofa, unable to eat or go out. Anxious, frightened thoughts teemed in my head. I felt overwhelmed by fear and began to contemplate suicide. In desperation I whispered, 'Dear God, please help me!'

Later, I noticed our church magazine on the coffee table. I opened it and my eyes fell on the words of a poem: 'Remember, God loves you.' For a moment the world stood still. I read the poem over and over until I knew it by heart. This comforted me, and I began to search for other similar things that 'spoke' to me, beginning with hymns I had learned at school. The concentration I needed to learn the words by rote filled my head and blocked out my previous, frightening thoughts.

God healed me and became the centre of my life. A short time later the minister of our church gave me my first copy of *The Upper Room* and I began to read it daily. I am well, happy and busy, and I try to serve the Lord in any way I can. To others suffering from mental illness, I would say: reach out to God and ask for his help. He can and will lead you out of darkness and into the light.

Prayer: *Dear Lord, when we reach out to you in fear and anxiety, thank you for your abundant love, which heals, comforts and gives us peace. Amen*

Thought for the day: I will let God heal my heart and my mind.

Shirley Smith (Hertfordshire, England)

PRAYER FOCUS: THOSE SUFFERING FROM MENTAL ILLNESS

Enjoying God

Read Psalm 84:1–12

Better is one day in your courts than a thousand elsewhere; I would rather be a doorkeeper in the house of my God than dwell in the tents of the wicked.

Psalm 84:10 (NIV)

As a child I loved going to my grandma's house. She lived four hours away, yet she always had cinnamon rolls fresh from the oven when we arrived. I picture myself sitting at her kitchen table, surrounded by my brothers and sister, with icing dripping down our chins.

We kids loved our grandma, but the first thing we always wanted to do after finishing our cinnamon rolls was to go see Grandma's friend Ruth. Ruth was funny, and we loved spending time with her. As an adult, I sometimes think back on those visits and wonder how Grandma felt when we dashed off to see Ruth. Was she sad? Did she think we loved Ruth more than we loved her? The truth is that we loved Grandma but we thought Ruth was more fun.

Unfortunately, we sometimes feel the same way about God. We love God; but daily concerns seem to be more fun, so we cut short our time with him. I would like to visit with Grandma a little longer, but she is gone. However, the Lord is still here, longing to spend time with me, just as Grandma did. God wants to spend time with you, too.

Prayer: *Dear God, show us what it means to delight in your presence, and teach us how to love you. Amen*

Thought for the day: Cherish your time with God.

Barb Raveling (Montana, US)

Designed for Life

Read 1 Corinthians 15:51–58

'Where, O death, is your victory? Where, O death, is your sting?'… But thanks be to God, who gives us the victory through our Lord Jesus Christ.
1 Corinthians 15:55, 57 (NRSV)

In recent years, several family members have entered the fading years of life, and others have died. I can do little to aid them and nothing to prevent their death. I realise my powerlessness in the face of death and feel caught in the grip of weakness, unable to help those I love or even myself. In these times, I bear in mind that God did not design us for death but for life.

Death stalks all of us, young or old, waiting to snatch away our final breath. But when death draws close to me and my family, I remember that this is not the end, that goodbye does not last for ever, and that closing eyes will open again. I may be powerless to overcome death, but my Redeemer, Jesus Christ, has conquered death—and my hope is in him!

Prayer: *Heavenly Father, strengthen our faith so we can hold on to our hope in you even in the face of death. Empower us to live today by your power that raised Jesus from the dead. Amen*

Thought for the day: Because Christ lives, we also live; death is not the end.

Titus O'Bryant (Texas, US)

Always Home

Read Psalm 139:1–10

Lord, you have been our dwelling place throughout all generations.
Psalm 90:1 (NIV)

When someone asks our sons where they are from, they have no quick and simple answer. This is because their father's career sent our family packing every few years—from Hawaii to California to Texas to Virginia and several points in between. We really have no place we can call our home town.

Yet in all these places we consistently felt the presence of God, finding our true and permanent home among fellow believers. The buildings, sizes of the congregations and worship services varied; and the local speech patterns and accents changed. But these differences were slight compared with the common bond we shared. The fellowship we find with God's people has given us stability, comfort and security wherever we have lived.

Society seems more transient than ever with continual changes in location, careers, health, financial circumstances and family structure. Few people manage to live long without enduring some major life changes and the stresses that come with them. Like the Israelites who wandered in the wilderness, we may feel as if we are strangers in this world. What a comfort to know that we cannot move beyond the reach and love of God!

Prayer: *Dear Lord, help us to feel your presence wherever we go and to find our true home in your love, with your people. Amen*

Thought for the day: Wherever life may take us, God has been there before us.

Julia Denton (Virginia, US)

A Measure of Grace

Read Ephesians 4:11–16
Each of us was given grace according to the measure of Christ's gift.
Ephesians 4:7 (NRSV)

Recently I planted two ornamental plants. The larger one I planted in a big pot to allow it room to grow. The other I planted in a much smaller pot, expecting it to remain small. What a surprise to watch how the plants grew! The once-smaller plant flourished and grew larger than the first, while the other remained about the same size.

Our spiritual growth can be something like the growth of my plants. As believers, we each have a measure of grace and have been blessed by God. But each of us relates to God differently so, as with my plants, our growth in the Christian life can be very different.

Some of us remain the same for years, attending church and giving, growing little if at all. Others try new ways of serving and giving, and they grow as Christians. The apostle Paul instructs us to nurture our faith: 'Grow up in every way into him who is the head, into Christ… as each part is working properly, [it] promotes the body's growth in building itself up in love' (Ephesians 4:15–16).

Prayer: *Loving God, guide and teach us to live your truth in love so we may continue to grow. Amen*

Thought for the day: How am I nurturing my spirit every day?

Magdalena Alvarado Guajardo (Coahuila, Mexico)

Disaster

Read Psalm 46:1–5

O God… I will take refuge in the shadow of your wings until the disaster has passed.

Psalm 57:1 (NIV)

From time to time our world is shaken by the powerful forces of earthquakes, tsunamis, hurricanes and fires. These events often cause the deaths of thousands. Afterwards, many attempt to explain these tragic events as God's punishment, while others ask the classic question: 'Why?' The psalmist also struggled in the face of tragedy, describing life in terms of darkness and despair, but also holding out the hope of God's salvation and deliverance.

In fact, this psalm can be our prayer, too, in the midst of life's tragedies. We want someone to remember our plight. We want the assurance that we are not forsaken but that God will come to our aid.

Our world will never be free of disasters, but even amid life's storms we can rest assured that God does not forsake those in need. And we can also resolve to take part in rescuing them.

Prayer: *God of creation, we ask that in the midst of our tragedies you will be present with us and comfort us. Sustain us also as we help others. Amen*

Thought for the day: Even though we may feel abandoned, God is near to us in our pain.

Link2Life: *Contact someone you know who is struggling with life at the moment.*

Todd Outcalt (Indiana, US)

Getting Rid of the Barnacles

Read Hebrews 12:14

The fruit of the Spirit is love, joy, peace, patience, kindness, goodness, gentleness and self-control. Against such things there is no law.
Galatians 5:22–23 (NIV)

On a visit to a turtle rescue centre, I marvelled at the great variety of turtles. They ranged in size from three inches to three feet, all swimming happily in their assigned tanks—many of them with only one flipper or one eye.

Several turtles swimming in a fresh-water tank particularly intrigued me. On their shells were barnacles that had attached themselves to the turtles and had flourished in salt water. The effects of these barnacles can range from stress to the turtle, due to increased surface drag when the turtle swims, to more serious damage from bacterial or fungal infections. However, now that these turtles had been transferred to fresh water, the barnacles were no longer being nourished and so would eventually disappear.

Like those turtles, we are sometimes weighed down by burdens. Whether out of indifference, ill nature, being with the wrong crowd or ignoring God's nudges, we create an environment that feeds the 'barnacles' of resentment, hatred, irreverence, jealousy, materialism and other damaging traits. But if we change our spiritual environment, the attitudes of our sinful nature will no longer thrive. When we live in an environment shaped by God's word and surrounded by his people, we can focus on the fruit of the Spirit.

Prayer: *Gracious God, lead us onto the paths that help us to live the life you plan for us. Amen*

Thought for the day: What 'barnacles' keep me from living fully for God?

Gretchen Stults (New Jersey, US)

A New Heart

Read Ezekiel 36:24–28

Create in me a clean heart, O God, and put a new and right spirit within me.
Psalm 51:10 (NRSV)

I saw a television news story about a 68-year-old Israeli man who, after ten years of serious heart disease, had received a heart transplant. The donor was a young Russian man who had died in tragic circumstances. He had been killed on the street.

A year after the operation the man was able to meet with the mother of the person who had given him life. The meeting was very emotional. The woman asked if she could press her ear to his chest so that she could hear the beating heart of her son.

I was also dying in a spiritual sense. But 20 years ago I had a heart transplant. Here is how the prophet Ezekiel described my operation: 'A new heart I will give you, and a new spirit I will put within you; and I will remove from your body the heart of stone and give you a heart of flesh' (Ezekiel 36:26).

My donor, my Saviour who gave his life for me, is Christ Jesus. He also died in tragic circumstances. He was killed on the street. I received from my donor a new heart. Now the heart of my Saviour beats in my chest, and I sing praises to the risen Christ!

Prayer: *Lord Christ, you saved us. You gave us eternal life. Praise and glory to you forever. Amen*

Thought for the day: Listen for Jesus above the noise of the world.

Irina Ivanova (Pskov, Russia)

Where is Your Samaria?

Read Luke 6:27–36

Jesus said, 'You will receive power when the Holy Spirit has come upon you; and you will be my witnesses in Jerusalem, in all Judea and Samaria, and to the ends of the earth.'

Acts 1:8 (NRSV)

I think Jesus deliberately included Samaria in the commission given in today's quoted scripture. Jews and Samaritans didn't get along. In fact, Jews of Jesus' time avoided travelling through Samaria even if it meant a much longer journey. Samaritans were people Jews wanted to avoid. So it could not have been an accident that Jesus told the disciples to reach out to them.

Considering this, I ask myself, who are the Samaritans in my life? We live in a fractious and hateful time, one filled with harsh language that often vilifies people who are on the other side of an issue. But Jesus demonstrated a different way. He went through Samaria, not around it. He visited with a Samaritan at a well (see John 4). He held up a Samaritan as a model for being a true neighbour (see Luke 10). In other words, he looked for opportunities to build bridges of understanding and love rather than building walls of division.

Where is my Samaria? That's where I need to go. Am I building bridges of understanding and love, as Jesus calls me to do, or am I saying and doing things that help to build walls of separation?

And what about you? Where is your Samaria?

Prayer: *Dear Jesus, help us to follow your command and reach out in love to those we would rather avoid. Amen*

Thought for the day: Where is Jesus sending me?

Dan Johnson (Florida, US)

Soul Tonic

Read Psalm 119:129–135

Their delight is in the law of the Lord… They are like trees planted by streams of water, which yield their fruit in its season, and their leaves do not wither.
Psalm 1:3 (NRSV)

As I am now getting older, I have set a goal to read more. My favourite reading material is the Bible. I firmly believe reading scripture keeps my mind fresh and revitalises my soul. For my daily devotional reading time, I study the passages related to the day's lesson, though often I read them in a hurry. However, when I want to meditate on those passages, I make it a point to start with a brief prayer. Then, with a dictionary nearby to help me find meanings of words, I delve more deeply into the scripture. I take my time, often rereading a certain text several times to understand what God is saying to me.

I find this reading to be a tonic for my soul. My thoughts continue to be nourished by the stories and promises of God—promises that require my commitment so that his work will be fulfilled in me. My prayer is that God's Spirit will dwell in me and guide my actions as I live each day obedient to what I hear as I reflect on God's word.

Prayer: *Thank you, God, for your word. Grant us hunger to read it more and joy as we read. In Christ's name. Amen*

Thought for the day: Reading scripture revives the soul.

Link2Life: *Make a new start on reading the Bible with greater attention.*

Maria Refugio Quevedo (California, US)

Throw it Away?

Read Hebrews 11:1–7
Now faith is confidence in what we hope for and assurance about what we do not see.
Hebrews11:1 (NIV)

The African violet on top of my refrigerator had bloomed, and the purple flowers were beautiful. My son gave me the plant when he was eight years old, and the violet had never bloomed before. Many times over the years I thought I would throw it away because of its hopeless condition, but I didn't.

Tears ran down my face as I thought about what God had done for my son. Five months earlier, he had entered a Christian recovery centre for drug addicts. The transformation God has made in his life is miraculous. Jeremiah 29:11 says that God plans a future for us that is good and full of hope. I compared my son to the violet. As I had cared for the plant over the years, I had cared for my son by praying for him. Eventually, life and beauty came forth from both.

If we throw away our hopes and dreams because the situation looks grim or change takes too long, we may miss what God is about to do. When we continue to trust, he works faithfully to accomplish good.

Prayer: *Eternal Father, you promise that the desert will blossom and we will see your glory (Isaiah 35:1–2). Help us by faith to see life where there is death, hope where there is fear and your beauty in our life. Amen*

Thought for the day: In God's kingdom, each of us will blossom and bear good fruit.

Suzanne Cooper (Missouri, US)

PRAYER FOCUS: FAMILIES OF THOSE WITH ADDICTIONS

Losing Things

Read Luke 15:3–6

For the Son of Man came to seek out and to save the lost.
Luke 19:10 (NRSV)

I scribbled some notes on a scrap of paper, planning to tidy them into an article. Later on, when I was ready to start work on it, I looked for my notes but, search as I might, I couldn't find them. Losing things is a frequent occurrence, I'm afraid. I forget where I've left my purse, I can't find a pen when I want one, and other items seem to vanish into thin air!

When our children were at home, there was the 'lost sock syndrome', when one sock of a pair went missing, and I ended up with a bag of odd socks, the others apparently having fallen into an eternal black hole. Frequently, when it was time for the children to set off for school, panic set in. Where was the gym kit, the pencil case, last night's homework? Always something vital went missing.

The good news is that God does not lose us, although we might try at times to lose him, and go our own way. But as in the parable Jesus told, the shepherd goes out and searches until he finds the lost and wandering sheep, and gently and lovingly takes it home. This is a picture of Jesus, our Good Shepherd, seeking us, his lost sheep, until we are found. How reassuring that God does not rely on our fallible memories!

Prayer: *Dear Lord, we thank you that you came to earth to save us when we were lost, and that you will never lose us. Amen*

Thought for the day: Jesus will never let us be lost, but will come to find us and bring us home.

Anne Rasmussen (Somerset, England)

Faithful Hearts

Read Acts 1:12–26

The King will answer them… 'Just as you did it to one of the least of these who are members of my family, you did it to me.'
Matthew 25:40 (NRSV)

My daughter asked, 'Mum, who took Judas' place after he died?' I answered confidently, 'Matthias.' She considered this for a moment, then asked, 'What did he ever do for Jesus?' I was stumped by the question of a six-year-old.

I searched the Bible for other mention of Matthias' name but found nothing. However, when the disciples were discussing Judas' replacement, they chose from those who had been with the group since the baptism of Jesus until the day that he ascended into heaven. They narrowed it down to two people, Justus and Matthias. Why were they considered? Scripture tells us that they had been with the group from the beginning; they were faithful—not flashy, just faithful.

Taking a meal to an ill person, visiting someone in prison, serving in the church, volunteering to help with a holiday Bible club, or spending time in prayer for church leaders may not seem like much. But these acts meet needs in the kingdom of God. God isn't looking for people who make headlines; he is looking for those with faithful hearts. So, to paraphrase my daughter's question, 'What are you doing for Jesus?'

Prayer: *Dear Lord, sometimes our efforts seem small. Help us to realise that anything we do to help someone in need is done for you. Amen*

Thought for the day: What are you doing to honour Christ?

Diane Godair (North Carolina, US)

Bought with a Price

Read 1 Corinthians 15:1–11

You were bought with a price; therefore glorify God in your body.
1 Corinthians 6:20 (NRSV)

Some time ago I got the frightening news that my first cousin had been kidnapped. His kidnappers asked for a ransom. I could not believe it. What I read about only in newspapers had come to my doorstep. The immediate and extended family lovingly contributed their money to save our captive cousin. The ransom was paid, and he was set free. We all rejoiced.

This experience made me think about the ransom Jesus Christ paid for the salvation of our souls. The price Christ paid for us became real to me as I thought about what my cousin went through and how we had to buy him back with a price. How could we ever pay for such a gift?

People say that salvation is free. It is free to us; however, Christ has paid a dear price for us. Even when we were sinners, Jesus Christ was willing to die for us.

Prayer: *Dear God, thank you for sending Jesus to ransom us. Help us to remember that we belong to you. As Jesus taught us, we pray, 'Our Father which art in heaven, Hallowed be thy name. Thy kingdom come. Thy will be done in earth, as it is in heaven. Give us this day our daily bread. And forgive us our debts, as we forgive our debtors. And lead us not into temptation, but deliver us from evil: For thine is the kingdom, and the power, and the glory, for ever.'* Amen

Thought for the day: Jesus showed us the worth of each soul.

Foluke Bosede Ola (Nigeria)

Hope Lives

Read Luke 8:40–55

[Jesus] said, 'My child, get up!'… and at once she stood up.
Luke 8:54–55 (NIV)

Over 40 years ago, when my oldest daughter was less than three weeks old, her paediatrician told us, 'Stay in town. Hope won't live through the night.' (We lived more than 50 miles from the hospital, over country roads.)

Hope had been born with a flawed digestive tract. She did not tolerate any nourishment, not even her mother's milk. Her doctor had tried all the options to cure her, but nothing worked. Hope had lost too much weight. She was dying. The next morning my wife was too distraught to go to the hospital. Wracked with sorrow, tears blinding me, I drove with a friend from theological college who tried to convince me that even in the valley of death God is with us. I would not be consoled.

I went into the hospital expecting news of Hope's death and could not understand what I saw: her paediatrician was positively giddy with happiness. 'It's a medical miracle!' he gushed. 'Hope is alive!'

Every Good Friday, I relive the feelings of that day long ago as I think about the death of Jesus. The world is without hope. Jesus is dead. I picture evil dancing in joy. But we know Easter is coming. Praise God. Jesus is alive!

Prayer: *Thank you, God, for Easter. We praise you that you work your miracles in and through us today. In the name of Jesus, our resurrected hope and joy, we pray. Amen*

Thought for the day: In the face of deaths large and small, Easter promises us life.

Gary Meader (Missouri, US)

A Divine Rescue

Read Acts 12:1–17

To him who by the power at work within us is able to accomplish abundantly far more than all we can ask or imagine, to him be glory.
Ephesians 3:20–21 (NRSV)

Each time I read about Peter's release from prison, I smile. The scene opens with Peter sleeping so soundly that the angel has to poke him to wake him up. Once Peter is free, he visits those who have been praying for him. Rhoda, who answers his knock, is so excited to hear him that she doesn't let him in! He is left waiting while she tries to convince the people praying for him that he's outside. But they are quicker to believe in a visit from an angel than in a divine rescue.

What were these believers praying for? If they were praying for Peter's rescue, they failed to believe God had answered them. Were they praying without believing, or were they asking for something less than the rescue that God wanted to grant?

We have all prayed for something we didn't get—healing from an illness, a job that went to another person or some other good. At such times we can become timid about asking again, so we ask for a small favour instead of what we really want. We don't want to be disappointed. I may never understand why I sometimes see no answer, but I do understand that the cost of praying only small prayers is too high. God may not grant me many miracles, but how many will I see if I never ask?

Prayer: *Thank you, God, for sometimes giving us big answers that we didn't have the courage to ask for. Please help us to trust you enough to make our requests as big as you are. Amen*

Thought for the day: God is big. Are my requests too small? Think about your prayers for others: are they big enough?

Jennifer Aaron (Washington, US)

Judging Others

Read Romans 14:1–12

Who are you to pass judgment on servants of another? It is before their own lord that they stand or fall.

Romans 14:4 (NRSV)

My husband and I travelled to Israel with a Christian tour group. On the eighth day of our trip, we visited the Temple Mount in Jerusalem. The Western Wall is a massive limestone wall where people come to pray.

Men, women and children of all ages and different religious traditions, dressed in all types of garb, were slowly moving to and from the wall. As I made my way to the wall to insert my prayer list in one of the crevices between the stones, I noticed with great dismay a woman talking on a mobile phone. Just like home, I thought. Here we are in a holy place, and she's talking on the phone! Suddenly the woman moved the phone from her ear to the wall, held it there for a few moments, and then left quietly. She had been helping someone who couldn't be present to be part of praying at the wall with others. I had just witnessed an expression of the faith of two individuals and a loving act. I often recall this event, and I've recounted it to others on several occasions.

How many times in the course of a week or even a day do we judge before knowing all the facts? And for that matter, what right do we have to judge another at all?

Prayer: *Dear Lord, help us not to judge but rather to listen to and to help others. Amen*

Thought for the day: Love one another—and leave judgment to God.

Diane Haviland (New Jersey, US)

The Right Tools

Read 2 Timothy 3:14–17

Your word is a lamp to my feet and a light to my path.
Psalm 119:105 (NRSV)

I arrived at playgroup with my daughter and was asked to assemble some new furniture for the children. The screwdriver they gave me was too small and unsuitable for the job. It jumped out of the screw head several times and injured me. I went home and brought back more appropriate tools and completed the work without problem.

I often try to use the 'wrong tools' in life, too. I try to handle tasks in my own way, relying on my own experience and knowledge, without direction from God. Too often things don't work out; even worse, I get hurt. But when I use the right tools—reading and acting on the word of God and seeking his direction in prayer—I can complete my tasks with pleasure.

God has given us the tool of holy scripture as 'a lamp to [our] feet and a light to [our] path'. It is a primary tool to help us keep our life together and make us strong and useful for God's work.

Prayer: *Dear heavenly Father, we thank you for your word. Thank you that it gives answers to the questions we face and wisdom to preserve us from being overcome by the hurts and disappointments of life. Amen*

Thought for the day: The Bible is a useful tool as we face life's tasks.

Yevgeni Tarasov (Moscow, Russia)

Life's Seasons

Read John 3:1–17

Jesus [said], 'Very truly, I tell you, no one can see the kingdom of God without being born from above.'
John 3:3 (NRSV)

The day after my brother's funeral, a blizzard blew in with winds that whipped the snow into twisting funnels. That was in April. The following day I trudged through the cemetery. It all seemed surreal: my brother's death, me at his grave, and mounds of snow burying the flowers. Where was spring—the season we associate with rebirth, regeneration and resurrection?

When my brother died, I entered a season of severe depression. I was 40 years old and didn't attend church or even worship God. But God still heard my desperate cries for help. A desire to attend church came over me, and I began searching the telephone directory. I made an appointment with a pastor for grief/spiritual counselling. In compassion, God had led me there, and I entered a new season of life when I heard the gospel of salvation through Jesus Christ. My life and my spirit were transformed. I was born again.

Our loving and merciful God 'desires everyone to be saved and to come to the knowledge of the truth' (1 Timothy 2:4). No matter what we've done, God offers each of us rebirth through the death and resurrection of Jesus Christ. Hope, redemption and eternal life are God's priceless gifts to us.

Prayer: *Thank you, Father, for seeking us before we knew that we needed you. Amen*

Thought for the day: No one is beyond the reach of God's redeeming power.

Debra Pierce (Massachusetts, US)

Good Neighbours

Read Leviticus 19:15–18

If it is possible, as far as it depends on you, live at peace with everyone.
Romans 12:18 (NIV)

From the moment we moved in, we knew that our neighbours were going to be difficult. They argued loudly, their dogs barked, and their music blared at all hours.

Though we asked them to quieten down, our requests did little more than provoke them. Their lifestyle and values differed from ours, and nothing seemed to bridge the gap. So we chose to distance ourselves.

Weeks turned into years. Weary and frustrated, I asked God, 'Why aren't my prayers enough? Isn't this situation ever going to change?' Troubled, I searched the scriptures. I came across Jesus' admonition, 'Love your neighbour as yourself' (Matthew 22:39). The verse was familiar; but in my frustration and anger, I had forgotten that these neighbours were God's people, just as I am. God's words pierced my heart that day, reminding me to not only recite the commandments but to live them out.

My neighbours did not change, but my attitude toward them did; and we were able to live peaceably beside them.

Prayer: *Dear Lord, open our hearts to love those you have placed in our lives. Amen*

Thought for the day: Love as Jesus loves.

Link2Life: *Organise a get-together for the neighbours in your street.*

Deanna Baird (Michigan, US)

The Living Word

Read Psalm 91:1–16

[You] will say to the Lord, 'My refuge and my fortress; my God, in whom I trust.'

Psalm 91:2 (NRSV)

The woman I was visiting had asked me to read the psalm to her; so I should not have been surprised that as I read, she whispered the words, 'You who live in the shelter of the Most High, who abide in the shadow of the Almighty…'. When I stumbled in my reading, the words poured forth from her. She told me afterwards she had carried that psalm in her heart through some difficult days. She had been a refugee from a country torn by poverty and violence. After making a new life in the United States and starting a family, she was diagnosed with terminal cancer.

I was her hospice chaplain. I spent time each week reading to her and praying with her. I was new at the job, and she showed me that the words of scripture are themselves balm to a tired soul. I had read scripture in private devotion, Bible study and worship, but I had seldom read scripture when I visited those who were ill.

Now I read scripture during many of my visits. The word of God, without commentary or preaching, comes into our darkest valleys as a source of great comfort and peace—for my patients and for me.

Prayer: *Gracious God, thank you for your grace which we find in the words of scripture. Thank you for the comfort and healing you bring as we read and listen to your word. Amen*

Thought for the day: The words of scripture bring us hope and direction.

Avis Hoyt-O'Connor (Maryland, US)

Fully Human

Read Hebrews 2:9–18

We have [a high priest] who has been tempted in every way, just as we are.
Hebrews 4:15 (NIV)

Sometimes when talking with others I give examples of how Jesus responded when faced with circumstances such as we're discussing. The usual response to this is, 'Yes, but Jesus is God!'

We often think that Jesus had the unfair advantage of being God, that temptation had no effect on him, that he by nature would respond in the best possible way to bad situations. We prefer to concentrate on Jesus as God, but today's passage from Hebrews reminds us that Jesus was completely human, suffering as all of us do.

Jesus shared in our humanity. He struggled in the Garden of Gethsemane; he was betrayed by a close disciple. He endured public rejection and humiliation and the awful pain of flogging and crucifixion. Were all of these just God going through a charade? Was life easy for Jesus? No. Jesus experienced every sensation and every emotion, just as any of us would. However, in spite of it all, he remained pure and blameless. That is what makes the message so powerful. The gospel is not about how God effortlessly came to save us but how he became 'fully human in every way' (v. 17)—made like his brothers and sisters—and died to save us.

'Salvation is free,' we say. Yes, it is free for us to receive—but it came at great cost to the Giver.

Prayer: *Dear Father, forgive us when we take for granted your gift of salvation. Amen*

Thought for the day: Jesus shows us how to be fully human and available to God.

Derek Sum Wei Siang (Malaysia)

Christ Has Risen

Read Mark 16:1–8

Train children in the way they should go; when they grow old, they won't depart from it.

Proverbs 22:6 (CEB)

My grandmother came to Argentina from Russia, with painful memories of war. Her eyes had the appearance of being on the verge of tears that you could not wipe away. She left behind her parents and sister, never to see them again. Grandmother Xenia held on to her Slavic traditions as a way to remember her family.

As was the custom in my grandmother's native land, Holy Week was a busy time, with much preparation leading up to Easter—shopping, meal preparation and house cleaning. My grandmother lovingly prepared delicacies for the Easter meal—tea prepared in the samovar, *blini* (Russian pancakes), *kasha* (porridge), *kotlety* (meatballs), and most of all *pashka* (Russian Easter cheese dessert).

Finally, Easter Sunday would arrive and so did the true reason for our family celebration. We sat around the table where large cloth napkins were placed on top of the white tablecloth. My grandmother would raise her cup of tea and offer a greeting to the family with a gracious smile: '*Christos voskrese* (Christ has risen)!' And in one voice we responded: '*Voistinu voskrese* (Truly Christ has risen)!'

Many years have passed; family customs and traditions have changed; but we still honour the love and sacrifice of Christ.

Prayer: *Risen Lord, your sacrifice on the cross is an opportunity for us to demonstrate your love through our service. Amen*

Thought for the day: What act of service or kindness can I offer someone today?

Graciela Kupcevich de Cohen (Patagonia, Argentina)

Light the World

Read 1 John 1:5–7

Jesus said, 'You are the light of the world.'
Matthew 5:14 (NIV)

I collect flashlights of various shapes and sizes. I have a small one in my handbag, a large one in my car, a variety of old ones in my cupboards and several sturdy ones posted around the house in case of an emergency. Why collect flashlights? Because I feel afraid in the dark.

Because Jesus said he is the Light of the world, I know that wherever I go, whatever happens, I have the most powerful Light in the world with me and I need not be afraid of what the future holds. Christ is my source of light and, as his follower, I am to light up the world around me with love and grace.

We are different vehicles of the light of Christ, but each one of us has the responsibility and joy of bringing this light into a dark world. Together, we light the way to truth so others can find their way to God.

Prayer: *Dear God, in the darkness of our world make us conduits of the Light of the world shining into despair and corruption. Help us never to grow weary of being your light. In the name of Christ. Amen*

Thought for the day: When we are connected to Christ, our light can show others the way to hope.

Malinda Fillingim (Georgia, US)

Joyous Giving

Read 2 Corinthians 9:6–15

A tithe of everything from the land, whether grain from the soil or fruit from the trees, belongs to the Lord; it is holy to the Lord.
Leviticus 27:30 (NIV)

As a child, I saw that my parents believed in tithing. They gave ten per cent of their income to our church and to those who were needy. I remember my father often telling me, 'The more we give away, the more we get back.' At the time his words did not make sense to me. I couldn't understand how giving away money could result in having more.

But soon after my wife and I began tithing almost 20 years ago, we began to understand what my father had been telling me. The more we gave away, the more we received, from the standpoint of financial return but more importantly from the joy of knowing we had helped our church and God's children.

Whether our tithe is a small or large sum, the Lord is pleased with our offering. Attitude is just as important as the amount we give. And as we read in 2 Corinthians 9:7, God loves a cheerful giver!

Prayer: *Dear God, thank you for the resources you have given us. We pray that we will invest them in your work and service and that we will do so generously and joyfully. Amen*

Thought for the day: The more we give to others, the more we experience God's goodness.

George M. Smart (Ohio, US)

Why Don't You Help?

Read Colossians 1:15–23

Jesus cried out in a loud voice, 'Eli, Eli, lema sabachthani?' (which means, 'My God, my God, why have you forsaken me?').
Matthew 27:46 (NIV)

We had just finished a particularly busy Holy Week and Easter week-end when our 15-month-old son was injured. He pulled a tablecloth from a table, and the cloth brought with it a square, rough-cut glass vase that, as it fell, sliced his nose open. It was a serious cut.

At the hospital, we had to wait six hours for treatment because he needed an anaesthetic but had eaten just before the incident. His mother and I accompanied him into the operating theatre to keep him calm, but he panicked anyway. As the medical team strug-gled to hold the mask over his face long enough for the anaesthetic to take effect, they bumped his nose and started the bleeding again. Blood was everywhere; it even ran back into his eyes. With those blood-filled eyes he looked at me as if asking, 'Why are you standing and watching them hurt me like this? Why aren't you doing something to help me?' I told him was that this was the only way to 'make it better'.

Then it dawned on me: God watched Jesus being persecuted and dying on the cross, as Jesus asked, 'My God, my God, why have you forsaken me?' But Christ's death was God's only way to 'make it better', to heal us and to take away the pain and the penalty of our sin.

Prayer: *Lord God, thank you for your power and love made visible in Jesus. Thank you for his sacrifice that makes right our relationship with you. Amen*

Thought for the day: Jesus died to heal us of our sin and the pain it causes.

Gavin Campbell (Cape Town, South Africa)

Six Hours!

Read Mark 15:22–39

[Christ] bore our sins in his body on the cross, so that, free from sins, we might live for righteousness; by his wounds you have been healed.
1 Peter 2:24 (NRSV)

When I was young, the shops in our small town closed their doors from 12 noon to 3pm on Good Friday to commemorate the hours Jesus hung on the cross. My family sat through the entire three-hour service that rotated among the Baptist, Methodist and Presbyterian churches because they had the largest church buildings in the community. This observance was a formative experience in my life.

The cultural patterns of those days are long gone. We gave up the three-hour service decades ago in favour of a shorter service on Good Friday night, a tradition that goes back to the Middle Ages and one that I appreciate more every year.

But those childhood experiences conditioned me to think of Jesus as hanging on the cross only at that time of day. The Gospel of Mark, however, says that Jesus was crucified at 9am. Then midday darkness covered the earth from noon to three. I shuddered at the sudden awareness that Jesus was on the cross for six hours—an eternity in that hell. No wonder he prayed, 'My God, why have you forsaken me?' Who wouldn't feel God-forsaken at a time like that?

And yet Good Friday is not a time for theorising about how we are saved by God's love at the cross. Rather, it is a time simply to hear the story, to experience the love, and kneel in wonder in the presence of a God-forsaken God like this.

Prayer: *O God, thank you for your love that saves us from a God-forsaken eternity. In Jesus' name we pray. Amen*

Thought for the day: Relationship with Christ leads to the greatest love of all.

Jim Harnish (Florida, US)

A Tale of Three Tombs

Read Matthew 28:1–7

The angel said to the women, 'Do not be afraid; I know that you are looking for Jesus who was crucified. He is not here; for he has been raised, as he said. Come, see the place where he lay.'
Matthew 28:5–6 (NRSV)

Years ago I visited the tomb of Russia's Vladimir Lenin in Moscow and, later, China's Chou En-lai in Beijing. In each tomb, the body of the former leader was preserved in a clear coffin where his faithful followers could see it as they paid their respects. As I emerged from each of those tombs, the same thought went through my mind: Where could Jesus' followers go to see his body? The answer, of course, is nowhere!

I have also visited the Church of the Holy Sepulchre in Jerusalem, built around the traditional site of Jesus' tomb. I personally preferred another site, called Gordon's Garden Tomb. It was more how I imagined Jesus' tomb to be. I went inside past a large stone in a groove to permit rolling it to seal the tomb door. I saw where a body would have been laid. But there was no body in either of these two Jerusalem tombs.

No major religion except Christianity claims that its founder rose from death. If this claim by Jesus' followers had been false, all that the authorities would have had to do was point to his dead body. They tried to say his disciples stole it (Matthew 28:12–13), but would those who hid on Easter evening 'for fear of the Jews' (John 20:19) have later sacrificed their lives if they knew the resurrection was a lie? Three leaders, three tombs, but only one leader is alive today!

Prayer: *Thank you, God, for Christ our risen Saviour and for the imparting power of your Holy Spirit. Amen*

Thought for the day: Let us rejoice in our risen Lord!

Gus Browning (Texas, US)

God Knows My Name

Read John 20:1–16
[The shepherd] calls his own sheep by name.
John 10:3 (NIV)

As a child, I stood outside a railway station waiting to be collected by an aunt with whom I was to spend my holiday. I had not met her before; I had only seen her photograph. How would I find her in this bustling sea of people? Then I heard my name. That call was quickly followed by a smile and a hug from the aunt in my picture. I was somebody again in that crowd.

I imagine it was something like that for Mary from Magdala on the morning of Jesus' resurrection. The pre-dawn darkness would have accentuated the emptiness of her loss. Her face lined from weeping, the empty grave made her sorrow complete. In the growing light, even angels seemed unconvincing. And then she heard the risen Jesus say her name: 'Mary!'

For me, all the joy, the hope and the wonder of Easter comes with that meeting between Mary and Jesus. Death turns to life, endings become beginnings. But the best of all is recognising that in Jesus I can be sure God not only knows about me but knows my name. That is Easter. That is why Christ lived and died and rose again—so that each of us may know ourselves as deeply valued in the world's crowds.

Prayer: *Dear Lord, fill our lives with Easter moments of meeting you in the middle of everyday things and being sure you know our names, each one of us. Amen*

Thought for the day: For those who look and listen, every day is Easter.

Colin Harbach (Cumbria, England)

PRAYER FOCUS: THOSE WHO FEEL FORGOTTEN

Reflections

Read John 15:9–17

God so loved the world that he gave his only Son, so that everyone who believes in him may not perish but may have eternal life.

John 3:16 (NRSV)

'I know that my hair is sometimes questionable when I get out of bed in the morning,' my husband smiled as he walked into the kitchen for his morning coffee, 'but I just looked in the mirror, and what I saw almost frightened me!'

I smiled because I could certainly relate to what he was saying. Who hasn't looked in the mirror and been shocked, surprised or amused at what they saw? Mirrors play a very important part in helping us maintain our appearance, and what we see influences how we feel about ourselves. But there is something much more important than how we appear to ourselves and to other people. What if we could find a mirror that would allow us to see ourselves as God sees us?

Easter is the perfect reflection of how God feels about us. When we look at the cross, we see that he loves us enough to die to have a relationship with us. That tells us how much he values each one of us. When we look at the empty tomb, we see that no matter what happens God has the power to see us through anything—even death. Knowing this, we can face life with trust. Jesus came to show us God and to reflect his love for us (see John 14:8–9). Easter invites us to see ourselves worthy of redemption, loved beyond measure and created for eternal life!

Prayer: *God of the empty tomb, thank you for your love that is beyond understanding. Help us to see and love others and ourselves as you do. Amen*

Thought for the day: God looks at us with eternal love.

Susan McBride (Florida, US)

A Natural Response

Read 1 John 4:7–12
We love because he first loved us.
1 John 4:19 (NRSV)

I recently travelled with my sister to visit her daughter and grand-children. During our stay, I could not help but observe how much the children adored their grandmother. Five-year-old Kyler wanted to be with her constantly. When we sat down to eat, he insisted on sitting by Grandma. When we walked down the street, he held her hand. Near the end of the week, I asked him, 'Kyler, why do you love Grandma so much?' At first he shrugged and said, 'I don't know.' Then he suddenly brightened, as if the answer had just come to him, and exclaimed, 'Because she loves me!'

What a simple and honest answer! We all want to be loved, and we tend to love the people who love us. My sister would give her life for her grandchild, and he sensed the depth of her love. So it is with us. We do not love God in order to gain his love. We love God because he first loved us. Just as Kyler's love is a natural response to his grandmother's love, our devotion to God is a natural response to his great love for us.

Prayer: *Dear Lord, thank you for your love. May our love for and devotion to you be obvious to those around us. Amen*

Thought for the day: How am I expressing my love for God?

Debra Callaway (Kansas, US)

Christ is Risen!

Read Matthew 28:1–15

'Why do you look for the living among the dead? He is not here; he has risen! Remember how he told you… The Son of Man must be… crucified and on the third day be raised again.'
Luke 24:5–7 (NIV)

In our Bible discussion, we looked at the four Gospels' accounts of the resurrection of Jesus. We discovered that each of the Gospels reports a different version of how the events took place.

Even though there are different accounts of the resurrection, all four Gospels agree on one central truth: our crucified Lord overcame death and rose again after three days, as he had promised (Luke 24:7). To us who choose to believe, Christ's victory over death granted salvation and the right to become children of God (John 1:12).

As we celebrate and commemorate the risen Lord this Easter, I am comforted to know that we are all heirs of God's kingdom through the resurrection of Christ. We may come from different denominational backgrounds and see God's work differently, but we are all united in our joy as we celebrate the resurrection of Christ.

Prayer: *Dear loving God, thank you for the gift of salvation through your risen son Jesus Christ, whose resurrection we unite to celebrate. We honour you as we pray, 'Our Father which art in heaven, Hallowed be thy name. Thy kingdom come. Thy will be done in earth, as it is in heaven. Give us this day our daily bread. And forgive us our debts, as we forgive our debtors. And lead us not into temptation, but deliver us from evil.'* Amen*

Thought for the day: What does the Easter celebration mean to you?

Philip Polo (Nairobi, Kenya)

* Matthew 6:9–13 (KJV)

Answered Prayer

Read 2 Timothy 1:3–10

Let us consider how to provoke one another to love and good deeds.
Hebrews 10:24 (NRSV)

My family believes in God but will not attend church with me. At times, I become discouraged, and my own attendance becomes irregular.

One Sunday, instead of going to church alone, I decided to stay at home with my family. I was feeling sorry for myself and cried out to God about my loneliness and my longing for family worship. Not long after I had prayed, I heard a knock at the door. My brother stood there with his five-year-old daughter, Emma. He asked if she could go to church with me. Emma had got up that morning, dressed and told him that she wanted to go to church. My brother doesn't attend church; but he did not want to discourage Emma, so he drove the ten miles to my home to send her to church with me.

That day, I did not sit alone in church. As I held Emma's hand, I realised that God had spoken to me through this child. Emma helped me to feel not so alone. God showed love to both of us that day.

Prayer: *Almighty God, thank you for your love and care. Help us to see that sometimes our prayers are answered in unexpected ways. Amen*

Thought for the day: How has God answered my prayers?

Sue Rankin (Michigan, US)

From Depths to Surface

Read Luke 24:13–31

While [the two disciples] were discussing [all that had happened], Jesus himself arrived and joined them on their journey.
Luke 24:15 (CEB)

One day a whale surfaced from the ocean depths to swim beside our ship, watching us. For long minutes I looked into one of its huge eyes, knowing that I was seen as well as seeing. Then the whale disappeared into the deep, to surface in other times and places.

In a similar way God, who is always moving in the depths of existence, is revealed on the surface of life. Here the resurrected Christ shows us what is always true: that life is stronger than death and far more than meets the eye. The resurrection means that Christ Jesus continues to work in our depths, at times surfacing unexpectedly to be with us in unmistakable ways. In those moments we see and know that we are seen, and we sense our connection. Christ then returns to work in our depths, leaving us with the sure knowledge of his reality.

We do not know when Christ will make himself known, or what he does in the times we do not see him. But we do know that the risen Lord is present, whether on the surface or in the depths of our lives, transforming us beyond our understanding. And we cherish those moments when the resurrection is not just a doctrine but also a personal experience, when we look into the face of our Lord and know that we are not only seen but loved.

Prayer: *Gracious God, open our eyes to your presence and deepen our faith to sense it in our days. In Jesus' name. Amen*

Thought for the day: Christ works where we can see and where we cannot.

Jonathan Scott (Connecticut, US)

Two Fathers, One Love

Read 1 John 3:18–22

The Lord, the Lord, a God merciful and gracious, slow to anger, and abounding in steadfast love and faithfulness, keeping steadfast love for the thousandth generation, forgiving iniquity and transgression and sin, yet by no means clearing the guilty, but visiting the iniquity of the parents upon the children and the children's children, to the third and the fourth generation.

Exodus 34:6–7 (NRSV)

As a young girl, I was painfully shy and longed to be popular and outgoing. The girls in a newly formed 'club' invited me to join, to meet them at a local shop for the club initiation, and then to attend a sleep-over party. When we met at the shop, I learned that membership was earned by shoplifting. With a racing heart, I walked to a shelf that displayed Bible bookmarks, slipped a bookmark into my notebook, and returned to the pavement. The other girls questioned me, 'Well, what did you get?' I displayed my ill-gotten prize.

The party wasn't much fun for me. While the others chatted, I silently asked God's forgiveness. My parents had taught me to be honest. The next day, I confessed and my dad drove me back to the shop. I returned the bookmark and told Dad I would take my punishment. His comment was, 'You've punished yourself more than I would; you're forgiven.'

Like my earthly father, God loves us even when we stray and willingly forgives us.

Prayer: *Thank you, heavenly Father, for your love and mercy. Let the light of your love shine through us so that others may see and believe. Amen*

Thought for the day: God's love is a balm for the wounded.

Ann Coogler (South Carolina, US)

Thank You for Mustard

Read 1 Timothy 6:17–19

Every generous act of giving, with every perfect gift, is from above, coming down from the Father of lights, with whom there is no variation or shadow due to change.
James 1:17 (NRSV)

When my eldest daughter was five, she was learning to offer thanks at the dinner table. She began with the expected, 'Thank you, God, for this meal, and for my mummy and daddy.' She then proceeded to look around the table, adding, 'Thank you for mustard, and for pickles and hamburger buns, and for plates…' Although at first I found this merely a cute anecdote to share with friends, I've come to realise how meaningful her words really were.

In a world where food is scarce for many families, including some in my own community on the US/Mexico border, those of us who are able to place a nourishing meal on our table and look around at loving friends and family have reason to be deeply thankful. Even things we often overlook or take for granted—from condiments to cleaning supplies—may be a much-appreciated luxury to others.

I realise the importance of giving to local food banks, delivering or making meals for the housebound or contributing to other charities helping to feed the hungry. I continue to try to appreciate not just the 'big blessings' in my life but also the small gifts that make my days colourful and special.

Prayer: *Dear God, we thank you for our blessings. Help us to remember that all we have comes from you. Amen*

Thought for the day: Gifts from God are great and small.

Lisa Tate (New Mexico, US)

Freely Give

Read Matthew 13:1–8, 18–23

I planted, Apollos watered, but God gave the growth.

1 Corinthians 3:6 (NRSV)

Pahliwe is a young Xhosa woman who knows the Bible and is devoted to Jesus Christ. She lives in a homeless shelter in the Western Cape province of South Africa, but she longs to find work to support herself and make a home. I met her through my work with *The Upper Room*.

Pahliwe and others at this shelter have been using *The Upper Room* daily devotional guide for several months. This week on the train going into Cape Town to look for work, Pahliwe dozed off with the book on her lap. When the book fell to the floor, a man sitting next to her picked it up and began to read. When Pahliwe awoke, he asked if the book belonged to her. 'Well,' she said, 'it was mine, but now it is yours.' He was very pleased and said that he was so glad to have it as he travelled home to Zimbabwe.

Hearing this story, I imagined other ways God may use this little book. So I presented a thrilled Pahliwe with five new copies of *The Upper Room*—one for herself and four to give away to others.

As Pahliwe's story reminds us, as we go through our everyday routine, God can use us to serve others—even when we are unaware.

Prayer: *Dear God, help us to see what you are doing and equip us to serve you. Amen*

Thought for the day: Who needs to hear the message of scripture that sustains me day by day?

John Frye (Western Cape, South Africa)

Wherever We Are

Read Luke 15:11–24

Where can I go from your spirit? Or where can I flee from your presence?
Psalm 139:7 (NRSV)

The stranger spoke three words. What he said reminded me of God's presence, even to the depths of the seemingly bottomless pit I had hurled myself into. I tried to smile through my tears. I paid for my wine and left the shop, afraid the man would see the emotion his words had evoked. I couldn't tell you what he looked like because I couldn't face him without revealing my shame. But I do remember his words: 'Jesus loves you.'

At first, I wanted to snap back at him, 'I am well aware.' After all, my father was a preacher. I hadn't always been the snivelling wreck I had become, buying alcohol to drown my pain. Did he recognise the condition of my self-destructive soul? Did he understand the depth of his words? Through them, God was calling me back.

Over the next three years I often thought of his words. All that time, God, ever patient, was waiting for me. I began to pray, read scripture and worship with God's people. The moment I turned toward home, God was there to pick me up, to dust me off, to love me through the mess I had made of my life and to bring me back to the 'road that leads to life' (see Matthew 7:14).

Prayer: *Dear Lord, thank you for your presence and for your voice that calls to us wherever we are. Amen*

Thought for the day: Each person we meet needs to be reassured of God's love.

Rachel Noles (Tennessee, US)

Only the Good

Read Proverbs 15:1–4

Do not let any unwholesome talk come out of your mouths, but only what is helpful for building others up according to their needs, that it may benefit those who listen.

Ephesians 4:29 (NIV)

Every morning I write down a verse of scripture to remember as a motto for the day. One day my exhortation had to do with not slandering. I know that spreading rumours with the intention of harming someone is wrong.

But it occurred to me later that there is a form of speech as insidious as untruth: speaking of another's faults to a third person—even though the faults may be real. We are prone to tell others about the wrong someone has done or about a particular weakness someone struggles with. No lies are told. But such talk can cause prejudice or suspicion. Relationships can be negatively affected.

That day as I was reflecting on my motto from scripture, a work colleague telephoned to tell me a story that I was confident was not true. What was my first reaction? I will tell the others in my office about this! But doing so would have harmed the reputation of the person he was telling me about. Then I remembered the verse that I had read that morning and by the grace of God, I said nothing. Now I make it a practice to ask the Lord to watch over the door of my lips (see Psalm 141:3).

Prayer: *God of truth, give us the strength to speak only good about others. We pray with the psalmist, 'Set a guard over my mouth, O Lord' (Psalm 141:3). Amen*

Thought for the day: God calls us to speak words that heal, not hurt.

Ruth Nussbaumer (France)

Who Said 'Change'?

Read Matthew 25:31–40

The king will say, 'I was naked and you gave me clothing, I was sick and you took care of me, I was in prison and you visited me.'
Matthew 25:36 (NRSV)

Every week I volunteer at a young people's detention centre with others from my church. My goal when I joined this ministry was to change these young people and give them the tools they need to succeed in the world today.

Early on in my volunteer work, one of the former inmates was re-arrested (unfortunately, a fairly common occurrence). I saw that achieving my goal wouldn't be easy. As volunteers, we try to provide a positive influence for the youngsters as we talk to them about life and introduce them to passages of scripture that can guide them when they are released.

But how are we ever going to change them? Instead of becoming discouraged, I re-read the verse of scripture, Matthew 25:36, which inspired me to get involved in the first place. Jesus never said we had to change anyone. Whether we are meeting a stranger, a prisoner or someone who is ill, he gave us his direction. Visit. Spend time with them. I have to trust that God will work through us to reach these young people during our visits and beyond.

I try not to become discouraged when I learn that a former inmate is in trouble again. I return to the centre the next week to show unconditional love.

Prayer: *Dear God, help us to stop trying to change others. Use us instead to show your love and mercy. Amen*

Thought for the day: God sends us not to change people, but to love them.

Doug Caldwell (North Carolina, US)

In the Family

Read 1 Corinthians 10:31—11:1

Brothers and sisters, join in imitating me, and observe those who live according to the example you have in us.
Philippians 3:17 (NRSV)

'I can tell you are mother and daughter,' the sales assistant said. We smiled, making no comment. We've heard it before, and it always amuses us because we do not share DNA. My husband and I adopted our daughter when she was six weeks old.

So what makes us look alike? Living with me for 20 years, my daughter has picked up many of my characteristics. We think alike; our reactions are similar. In other ways we are quite different, but observers notice the ways in which we are the same.

When we are adopted into the family of God with Christ as our elder brother, something similar happens. We spend time with God and with other believers, we discuss important ideas and we gradually become more like Christ. We hope that when we go out into the world, people are reminded of God's love and compassion and want to follow Christ because of what they see in our lives.

Prayer: *Almighty God, help us to live so that people see Christ in us. In his name we pray. Amen*

Thought for the day: As God's children, we are meant to show the family traits of love and compassion.

Lanita Boyd (Kentucky, US)

The Small Stuff

Read Psalm 32:1–7

Create in me a clean heart, O God, and put a new and right spirit within me.

Psalm 51:10 (NRSV)

My aunt had to move because of declining health, and we put her house up for sale. The estate agent who came to value it saw what I had not seen: small carpet stains, a leaking tap, mould around a bath, a loose handle on a wardrobe and chipped paintwork. 'Those things seem small,' she said, 'but they make a huge difference in whether the house sells or not. Please get them fixed before we put up the For Sale sign.'

As I dealt with getting repairs done, God led me to begin to think about the 'small things' in my life—the bit of gossip I repeated, the minor resentments I hold on to, the way I sometimes shade the truth to my benefit, my pride and self-justification, judging the actions and worth of others. I wondered if these are actually sins.

Honestly, I knew that the answer is yes. I had committed sins and dismissed them as mere human failings. But they were sins and were obscuring the grace of God in my life.

In forgiveness and love, God helped me to be more honest and to confess my sins. His love and grace guided me through the period of helping my aunt and enabled me to begin a process of spiritual growth that led me to deeper faith and greater joy in my relationships.

Prayer: *Loving Father, we ask you to forgive us as we examine our consciences and confess to you the sins present in our daily lives. Thank you for your saving grace. Amen*

Thought for the day: God's grace extends to our deepest unconfessed sins.

Bettie Higgins (Alabama, US)

Philosophy and Faith

Read Acts 17:16–34

When they heard about the resurrection from the dead, some began to ridicule Paul. However, others said, 'We'll hear from you about this again.'
Acts 17:32 (CEB)

Several years ago in my college philosophy class, we studied the passage in the book of Acts that chronicled Paul's time in Athens. I was surprised to learn that discussion between Christians and philosophers was a far more ancient tradition than I imagined. To the Greek way of thinking, the professor explained, it was inconceivable that a god could die; gods were immortal and, therefore, could not die. At the conclusion of the lesson I was amazed by the image of Paul speaking of the resurrection and enduring the mockery of the philosophers. Even so, scripture says, 'Some people joined him and came to believe' (Acts 17:34).

Years later, I accepted Christ as my Saviour. I remembered the philosophy class, and I thought about how great the Lord truly is— to be immortal and the Supreme Being who not only died for us, but rose from the dead and lives today. This speaks to our sense of reasoning and to our spirit.

Many Christians view the resurrection as ancient history, perhaps as some did in my philosophy class. The resurrection happened over 2000 years ago, but Christ lives today. The resurrection is not another ancient story with a good moral to be remembered on Easter Sunday. The resurrection is the reality that sustains our faith and anchors our reasoning.

Prayer: *Risen Lord, may we not view the resurrection as ancient history, but rather the reality of our faith lived out day to day. Amen*

Thought for the day: The Lord has risen and lives today.

Enrique Acosta (Valencia, Spain)

PRAYER FOCUS: THOSE WHO DO NOT KNOW THE RISEN LORD

Strength in Weakness

Read 1 Corinthians 12:14–26

The members of the body that seem to be weaker are indispensable.
1 Corinthians 12:22 (NRSV)

Years ago I developed a painful and disabling spinal problem. I could no longer work, play or volunteer. Only appointments with doctors and various therapists broke up the long, lonely days at home. I felt that all my energy, time and money were focused on me and my body. It seemed that I had nothing left to contribute to the world.

Then, Paul's words in 1 Corinthians 12 changed my perspective: 'The members of the body that seem to be weaker are indispensable.' I marvelled at how God can turn the world's thinking upside down. God told me that I was valuable and needed just as I was, and helped me see that I had the opportunity to serve Christ by sharing his love with all the healthcare workers who were trying to help me. They could know Christ's love by the way I treated them. I could pray for them and their work daily.

An even greater insight, however, was that I was providing a way for them to serve Christ by helping me to heal. We need one another in the body of Christ. Weak and strong together, we can learn the importance of both giving and receiving God's love.

Prayer: *O God, sometimes it is difficult to accept care from others. Help us to accept graciously your love shown through others and to be grateful for opportunities to share it as well. Amen*

Thought for the day: No matter what our limitations are, we all can serve God by loving others.

Marilou Reed (Florida, US)

God's Favourite

Read John 10:11–16, 27–29

The Lord says, 'I have loved you with an everlasting love; I have drawn you with loving-kindness.'

Jeremiah 31:3 (NIV)

As she prayed for me, my friend said to God, 'Let Nancy know she's your favourite daughter.' 'God doesn't have favourites!' I thought. I knew he couldn't answer a prayer like that.

Later that day, I came across photos of my dear friend Doreen, who had died of bone cancer years earlier. I remembered her memorial service. As friends and family told stories about her, several women described themselves as Doreen's closest friend. They're mistaken, I thought. After all, I was her best friend. Doreen had so lavishly, unselfishly loved us all that each of us thought we were her favourite. She lived so well Jesus' commandment to love that I'd felt completely, unconditionally loved.

The Lord interrupted my memories, speaking gently in my heart, 'That's like my love.' I told him that I didn't understand. He said to me, 'You don't have to understand. Only believe.' And I do believe.

Still, I wondered how God could love me. I am certainly no saint. Then I remembered the stories of David—a liar, an adulterer and a murderer—and yet he was 'a man after [God's] own heart' (Acts 13:22). To my surprise, I realised that I am God's favourite. Each one of us is.

Prayer: *Dear God, thank you for your loving-kindness that draws us to you. Amen*

Thought for the day: I am God's favourite. And so are you!

Nancy Aguilar (Washington, US)

From the Back Seat

Read Colossians 3:12–17

Keep these words that I am commanding you today in your heart. Recite them to your children and talk about them when you are at home and when you are away, when you lie down and when you rise.
Deuteronomy 6:6–7 (NRSV)

Recently I was in my car, taking Marius out for some grandpa–grandson time. I was preoccupied. Usually, I would have played some children's praise music, but I had forgotten to turn it on. I heard Marius asking from the back seat, 'Where's our music, Grandpa?'

We manoeuvred through the traffic with the music playing, but again my mind wandered to work and the impossible deadlines I faced. I was resting my head on my hand when Marius asked, 'What's wrong, Grandpa?' Marius knew something was wrong. I told him I had a headache. Then I heard him praying, 'God, please help Grandpa to feel better. Amen.' We drove on a bit further. Marius spoke again, requesting a favourite Bible story, 'Tell me the story about Samuel, when he was sleeping.' I told the story. When Marius wanted to hear it again, I did a replay.

As we reached our destination, I realised that my grandson, not I, had been the teacher that day. I realised why Jesus told us to model our lives of faith on that of little children. If we praise God, if we identify the needs of others and pray for their hurts, if we love and tell the stories of faith, we will live well. I have made the Christian life way too complicated. To Marius, it is simple.

Prayer: *Dear God, teach us to live in your kingdom with the trust and simple honesty of little children. Amen*

Thought for the day: Every person in our lives can teach us something that God wants us to know.

Richard Lewis (California, US)

Turbulent Flight

Read Isaiah 43:1–4

Whatever is born of God conquers the world. And this is the victory that conquers the world, our faith.
1 John 5:4 (NRSV)

I frequently travel by plane, and generally the flights are pleasant. On one occasion, however, the pilot alerted us to buckle our seatbelts because we would be passing through an area of turbulence. The flight attendants started to move briskly about the cabin, and I tensed up with fear. I was not prepared for the strength of turbulence, and neither were the rest of the passengers. After what seemed an eternity, though in reality it was only a few minutes, the plane regained stability and I breathed a sigh of relief. As the pilot had said, the turbulence was localised.

Later, when I recalled this incident, I thought of our earthly life. The Lord does not promise us a life without strife. On the contrary, we will all go through bumpy times. However, when they come we can remember that we are only passing through some turbulence and God is with us. Faith steadies us.

Prayer: *Loving God, in all the challenges we encounter, stand by us and help us remain faithful to you. We pray as Jesus taught us, saying, 'Our Father which art in heaven, Hallowed be thy name. Thy kingdom come. Thy will be done, as in heaven, so in earth. Give us day by day our daily bread. And forgive us our sins; for we also forgive every one that is indebted to us. And lead us not into temptation; but deliver us from evil.'* Amen*

Thought for the day: God is with us when life shakes us and unsettles us.

Luis Alberto Jones (Trelew, Argentina)

Measuring Up

Read Ephesians 4:31—5:2

Speaking the truth in love, we must grow up in every way into him who is the head, into Christ.
Ephesians 4:15 (NRSV)

Recently while filling out job applications, I have completed several personality assessments. Many of these questionnaires have asked me to compare my own traits and abilities to those of the general population. After completing several of these surveys, I realised I had repeatedly chosen the response, 'I perform (a specific task) at least as well as most others.' This repeated response reminded me that I often use others as the gauge of my conduct.

The apostle Paul, in his letter to the church in Ephesus, reminds me that rather than comparing myself to those around me, I should strive to follow Jesus' example. His life is the perfect example for me to follow.

As ambassadors for Christ and children of God, we are called to be set apart, holy. God loves us and accepts us as we are, but we have a higher standard to aim for. I know I will never be sinless, but I can work to sin less as I look to Jesus as my role model. Rather than comparing myself to my peers, I now ask myself, How am I measuring up to Jesus' standard for my life? I want to seek first to please God rather than the people around me.

Prayer: *Dear Lord, thank you for sending Jesus as the perfect example for us to follow. Help us to be more like your Son so that we may better show you to others. In Jesus' name. Amen*

Thought for the day: When I grow up, I want to be like Jesus.

Julie Calleja (Michigan, US)

An Awful Year?

Read 1 Corinthians 15:1–8, 20

Christ has indeed been raised from the dead.

1 Corinthians 15:20 (NIV)

Although I am a lifelong Christian, I did not feel much like an immortal soul and did not have much confidence that I would rise to eternal life when medical tests revealed that I had cancer. But as I reflected on the Easter story, I found that I believed strongly in the resurrection of Jesus. And because Jesus rose, I had reason to believe that he would rescue me from death as well.

Out of gratitude, I began to pray more regularly. Perhaps because of my weak faith, I did not pray for cure of my cancer; but I did take time to praise God each day for what I had. Sometimes as chemotherapy and radiation took their toll, my prayers were little more than incoherent babbling. But with the aid of the Spirit, I kept praying (see Romans 8:26).

I endured months of treatments, underwent three major operations and had a colostomy for a while. My father died while I was going through all this. At the end of that awful time, my wife said, 'This must have been the worst year of your life.'

I thought about that for a minute, and I realised that throughout those difficult days I had been comforted with a profound sense of Christ's presence. 'You know,' I told her, 'it may have been the best.' Knowing Christ is with us transforms us and our struggles.

Prayer: *Dear God, help us to keep in our hearts the truth of your presence. Amen*

Thought for the day: God is the God of our Good Fridays, of life's awful trials, and also the God of Easter and resurrection.

Drew Sappington (Florida, US)

PRAYER FOCUS: THOSE WITH CANCER AND THEIR FAMILIES   119

'I'm Hungry!'

Read Matthew 5:1–12

Blessed are those who hunger and thirst for righteousness, for they will be filled.

Matthew 5:6 (NIV)

Four-year-old Brenda slipped unseen from her mother's pew. She walked down the aisle to the front of the church, where the minister stood making the weekly announcements. Taking his hand, she announced, 'I'm hungry!' Her embarrassed mother hurried to retrieve Brenda and bring her back to the pew. She assured the youngster that they would eat when they got home.

The little girl's statement stuck with me as the service continued. How many of us had come to church 'hungry' on this Sunday morning? Were the others in the congregation spiritually hungry for more of God? Was I? Had I entered the church expecting to be spiritually fed from the Lord's table?

Now each sabbath I make a conscious effort to come to church hungry. I wait expectantly for the Holy Spirit to feed my heart and soul. Then I continue my spiritual journey, nourished, invigorated and fed.

Prayer: *Lord, please increase our hunger and desire for you. In Jesus' name. Amen*

Thought for the day: How am I feeding my hunger for more of God?

Karen Wylie (Texas, US)

Wait on the Lord

Read Psalm 40:1–5

And now, O Lord, what do I wait for? My hope is in you.
Psalm 39:7 (NRSV)

One day at the close of my devotional time, I said a special prayer for my twelve-year-old son, Esteban. At the time, my wife was with our son at the hospital. At midnight, the phone rang. It was my wife, Doreen, with the news confirming that Esteban had meningitis. This was especially alarming because in those days in 1993 many young children had died from meningitis. I hung up the phone, fell to my knees and prayed. I placed Esteban in God's hands, as my wife and I had done countless times since his birth.

The next day a treatment plan for my son was started. Praying constantly, my wife and I placed our hope in the Great Healer to restore our son's health. God heard our prayers and the prayers of our brothers and sisters in the community of faith. After several months, Esteban pulled through.

Today Esteban serves God. He plays the piano in our worship services and is an English professor, deeply concerned for his students and their achievements. Doreen and I are grateful to God not only for restoring Esteban's health but also for the ways God is bringing wholeness to his Christian life. Our family has learned to wait on the Lord even in the midst of life's most challenging moments.

Prayer: *God of hope, may we always confide in you, especially in our darkest days. Amen*

Thought for the day: All that concerns me matters to God.

Raúl Rocha Gutiérrez (Buenos Aires, Argentina)

People Sharpeners

Read Hebrews 10:24–25 and 1 Thessalonians 5:12–22

As iron sharpens iron, so one [person] sharpens another.
Proverbs 27:17 (NIV)

The butcher I worked with in his shop showed me the best way to sharpen knives. I watched as he used a round metal file to sharpen not only his knives but his cleavers as well. Then he taught me the technique. Today I own a file, and my knives are always sharp.

The process of sharpening requires that iron meet iron. The friction wears away a dull edge to form a new one. My butcher friend told me that a dull knife isn't safe; it's actually more likely to cause serious injury. And a dull knife obviously doesn't do the job as effectively as a sharp one. So sharpening makes a tool more efficient and prepares it for the next job.

Similarly, our Christian friends can help us remain open to God's work in us. Their counsel may seem like unwanted friction at times, but we need friends who remind us of God's wisdom, keep us grounded in truth, and hold us accountable. Such accountability prepares us for the work God has for us to do.

Prayer: *Heavenly Father, thank you for Christian friends who love us enough to walk with us, pray for us and lead us into truth so that we can become like Christ. In Jesus' name. Amen*

Thought for the day: How has God used my Christian friends to 'sharpen' me?

Paula Geister (Michigan, US)

One Step Further

Read Matthew 4:18–22

How, then, can they call on the one they have not believed in? And how can they believe in the one of whom they have not heard? And how can they hear without someone preaching to them?
Romans 10:14 (NIV)

In my Bible study group, John requested prayer for his elderly neighbour, Sam, who had suffered a serious fall. John was helping by running errands for Sam. Our group leader prayed for Sam's health and also that John would have a chance to speak to Sam about Christ. Afterwards, John remarked, 'It never occurred to me to talk with Sam about Jesus.'

One person in our group said that helping Sam was, in fact, witnessing to him. And to be sure, it is. But another person said, 'Telling him about Christ goes one step further.'

That made me think. I enjoy visiting people who are sick or lonely, and I help by giving them lifts and meeting other needs. But how often do I speak to them about my faith? Do others know that I do these loving acts because Christ is my Saviour? Do they know what courage and strength and love Christ brings to my life?

Although I enjoy the friendships I make, my goal should be to draw people not to myself but to Christ by reading scripture or offering to pray. From now on, I want to go one step further and witness about my faith in Christ with words as well as deeds.

Prayer: *Dear God, help us to spread the good news of your love in words as well as deeds. In Jesus' name. Amen*

Thought for the day: Witnessing includes both words and actions.

Janice Davies (Illinois, US)

Winning Approval

Read Ecclesiastes 7:15–20

Do not be too righteous, and do not act too wise… Do not be too wicked, and do not be a fool.
Ecclesiastes 7:16–17 (NRSV)

When we were adolescents, my brother and I tried fiercely to win our dad's approval. This created a pattern of competition that continues to interfere with our relationship years later. During a recent country hike, my brother took the lead. The path wasn't especially difficult, and he set a frantic pace. Before long, however, he was gasping and suffering muscle cramps. We made it back safely, but that competitiveness made it difficult for us to enjoy our time together.

As a young Christian, I tried fiercely to win God's approval as well. I tried to be a perfect Christian: I tried to pray longer, I read the Bible more diligently and I behaved more piously than everyone else. That attitude, however, only alienated those around me.

When I read Ecclesiastes 7:15–20, I was appalled. How could someone be too righteous? And how could the writer suggest that we tolerate evil? Finally, I realised that, try as I might, I can never be perfect. I can live as pure and holy a life as possible and avoid pretension of righteousness, but I don't have to win God's approval. It's free and unconditional. I need only to accept it.

Prayer: *Dear God, may we always be aware that our good standing with you rests solely on your grace. Amen*

Thought for the day: Stop struggling and allow God to love you.

Thomas Dury (Colorado, US)

Taste and See

Read Psalm 34:1–10

How sweet are your words to my taste, sweeter than honey to my mouth!
Psalm 119:103 (NRSV)

Recently I was cleaning out drawers in my kitchen. In one drawer were recipe books and lots of cut-out recipes needing to be filed. Some of the recipes had been cut from magazines; some came from friends; some from my mother. I had had many of them for years, and most I had never tried. The dishes made from these recipes might taste fabulous, might even become family favourites. But I must make the dish and then taste the finished product.

My Bible is a bit like my recipe drawer. In it and in other notebooks, I have Bible verses written out, along with quotes from Christian writers and speakers. Most of these had great meaning for me at various times in my life.

Like the recipes, the word of God has to be 'tasted'—tried and acted on. Through the Bible God speaks to us, nourishes us, supports us. We are to read it regularly, with faith, and follow its wisdom. When a passage from God's word gets our attention, it is not meant to be a 'cut-out' word that we carry as a note to fall out of our Bible. Rather, each insight is something to meditate on and live until it becomes part of us.

Prayer: *Father God, thank you for your word, revealed in Jesus and made alive for us by your Holy Spirit. Thank you that your word is truth. Help us by faith to live it. Amen*

Thought for the day: By acting on the Bible's wisdom we taste God's goodness more fully.

Janice Ross (Orkney Islands, Scotland)

God's Angels

Read Matthew 6:25–34

Do not be anxious about anything, but in everything, by prayer and petition, with thanksgiving, present your requests to God.
Philippians 4:6 (NIV)

My husband has been out of work this past year. And this was not the first time; over the last 20 years he has been laid off five times. Each time has become more difficult for us as husband and wife and as a family. Our three children have endured many hardships and fears related to this. We've experienced days when there was no oil for heat or hot water. We've had empty food shelves and no electricity. For a time we were without a car, making it difficult to get to school, shops and church.

Even though we've experienced hardships, we've also received care by unexpected means. People have given us food, cars, money and their prayers and support. These people served as God's angels to us during these times, and we've learned to trust God to help us meet our needs. He has blessed us far more than the beautiful lilies Jesus described. When we know and accept God's love, we can face tomorrow's challenges with confidence that all will be well.

Prayer: *Loving God, thank you for your love and care shown through your children around us. Teach us in return to be willing to help others in their need. In Jesus' name we pray. Amen*

Thought for the day: How can I help God meet someone's need today?

Deborah Jones-Norberto (New York, US)

Sing God's Praises

Read Psalm 69:30–32

Make a joyful noise to the Lord.
Psalm 100:1 (NRSV)

The Lord did not bless my father with a pleasant singing voice. Quite the opposite: Dad couldn't carry a tune even if it had handles on it. Standing next to him in church made singing hymns difficult. My mother sang in the choir. My sister and I often shared a hymn book with Grandma, leaving Dad to howl in solitude at the other end of the pew. This never seemed to bother him. Each service found him enthusiastically adding his dissonant voice to the great hymns of the faith. He truly did make a 'joyful noise'—every Sunday.

The quality of our vocal efforts is not important to God. He doesn't care if we sing like angels or bleat like goats. He who created us knows our abilities. The act of praise from those who love God pleases him. When we sing in worship, we aren't performing for the approval of the people around us. We're lifting our voices to please God, who loves us, cares for us and died for us.

Prayer: *Dear Lord, may our songs, words, thoughts and deeds always praise you. As Jesus taught us, we pray, 'Our Father in heaven, hallowed be your name, your kingdom come, your will be done on earth as it is in heaven. Give us today our daily bread. Forgive us our debts, as we also have forgiven our debtors. And lead us not into temptation, but deliver us from the evil one.'* Amen*

Thought for the day: Praise God in everything you do.

Jacob Schneider (Maryland, US)

Faith Rather than Fear

Read Luke 12:13–21

Do not store up for yourselves treasures on earth, where moth and rust consume and where thieves break in and steal; but store up for yourselves treasures in heaven.
Matthew 6:19–20 (NRSV)

Today in my country, we are suffering from tremendous insecurity because of widespread violence. This has caused many of us to avoid owning cars or jewellery. Having these exposes us to the danger of losing our possessions or even our lives. Living under these extreme circumstances reminds us of Jesus' message not to store up treasures on earth but to seek rather the kingdom of heaven.

Even with all our precautions not to appear wealthy, a young man wielding a gun stole my wife's car. Thankfully my wife was not harmed, and the thief did not take her purse or the keys to our house. However, we have not been able to forget this incident. My wife reminds me, 'We did not lose only the car; we lost our security and sense of peace.'

Today, we live modestly out of necessity rather than conviction. The disciples of Jesus went a step further. For their faith, they left everything they knew to seek the kingdom of heaven. Our challenge is to nurture our spiritual growth and to place it ahead of an absurd accumulation of riches—to act out of faith rather than fear.

Prayer: *Faithful God, give us strength to place you first in our lives, above all that we own. In the name of Jesus Christ we pray. Amen*

Thought for the day: No possession is as valuable as our faith in God.

Magdiel Martinez (Nuevo Leon, Mexico)

Marvelling

Read Psalm 104:24–33

God saw everything that he had made, and indeed, it was very good.
Genesis 1:31 (NRSV)

A retreat I attended a few summers ago was in a setting that offered mountains, forests and a nearby lake—perfect places to explore God's creation. Before we ate our first midday meal, our retreat leader suggested that we spend our early-afternoon break wandering and relaxing in the area surrounding our cabins. 'Go marvelling,' she said. 'Find something in nature to bring back with you.'

When we gathered that evening, we placed on our worship table the items we had found during the afternoon: feathers, leaves, oddly-shaped tree branches, seedpods, wildflowers and rocks. We told the stories of our discoveries and celebrated God's gifts. The gift of marvelling at the works of our Creator energised us and brought us together.

From that experience, I learned that I can go marvelling almost anywhere. When I see a brilliant red, orange and gold sunset, I marvel. When I hear a bird singing, I marvel. When the air smells clean and the world grows still with the first snowfall of the season, I marvel. When fluffy clouds billow in the afternoon sky, I marvel. Sometimes I let the busyness of the day interfere with enjoying nature's beauty, but I try to save part of every day to pay attention to God's 'wonderful works'.

Prayer: *Loving God, draw our attention every day to your marvellous works, and keep us mindful of our role as caretakers of all that you have created. Amen*

Thought for the day: How will I make time to marvel at God's creation today?

Judith Olivia Jolly (North Carolina, US)

Small Group Questions

Wednesday 2 January

1. What is your earliest memory of a place? Is the memory partial or fairly detailed? Why do you remember this place?

2. How many times have you moved in your life? Where have you lived/did you live longest? Which places evoke the strongest memories?

3. What is hardest about moving? What is easiest? How long, and what, does it take to feel truly at home in a new situation—home, job, church? Why?

4. If you have changed churches or denominations or seriously considered doing so, why? If you have never done either, what might cause you to do so?

5. Looking back five to ten years, what spiritual changes do you see in yourself? What was/were the catalyst(s) for them? Were you aware of the changes while they were underway, or do you identify them only in looking back?

6. What are you doing/can you do to 'make [a] home' for God in your life? What will you do about this in the coming week?

7. The apostle Paul says that he has 'suffered the loss of all things' and encourages us to 'forget what lies behind' in order to gain the 'heavenly call of God in Jesus Christ' (Philippians 4:8, 13–14, NRSV). What have you left behind to pursue a life in Christ?

Wednesday 9 January

1. What do you think (or know) it feels like to be adopted literally? How might these feelings apply to being adopted into God's family?

2. Who in your congregation has adopted children? Why are we more open about adoption now than in earlier generations?

3. How might or does your community of faith reach out to children who do not have families? How is doing so a way of serving Christ?

4. What would you say is your family's 'name' in traits, behaviour or attitudes? For example, 'The Joneses are hard workers' or 'We believe in education' or 'We are Methodists' (or singers or animal lovers)? How do you live up to or contradict this family name?

5. How has God changed your 'name'? What fundamental changes has your faith made in you? What might others have said was your old name?

6. Read 2 Corinthians 5:14–21. In what ways do you live as a 'new creation'? What change would you like God to make in you spiritually, and why? How could you co-operate with him in changing? Or do you really not want to?

7. What evidence does your congregation give the community around your church that you are followers of Christ? How do you represent the family name Christian?

Wednesday 16 January

1. Had you heard of 'phantom pain' before this reading? If so, what do you know about it? If not, what questions are raised for you by hearing about it?

2. Do you have a high or low tolerance for pain? What causes you to answer as you do?

3. Can attitude affect our level of pain, making it seem less or more? What examples can you give to support your answer?

4. Whom do you know who lives with chronic pain? What is the effect of managing chronic pain?

5. Is Tracy's difficulty in feeling forgiven easy or difficult for you to understand? Why? What would you say to her if she were visiting your group?

6. What good purposes could guilt serve? When is guilt pointless, and how can we get rid of it in those situations?

7. Is dealing with guilt different for Christians than for non-Christians? If so, how? If not, why not?

8. 'When our hearts condemn us… God is greater than our hearts.' What advice would you give those whose heart is 'condemning' them?

Wednesday 23 January

1. What part do organised sports play in the life of your community? What is good about being part of sports events? Aside from physical injuries, how can participation be harmful?

2. Is competition contrary to Christian faith? What makes you answer as you do?

3. What are you passionate about—involved in frequently, giving lots of time and energy to? What do you get from your involvement? If your answer involves your faith, how did you come to be so involved?

4. Who do you know who is passionate about their faith? In what ways can passion for Christ be expressed? Is one way better than another?

5. What might keep someone from wanting to be passionate about faith and the church?

6. If those who know you best were asked whether you experience your faith more through your head (reading and studying), your heart (feelings, worship, prayer), or your hands (acting, doing), which would they say, and why? In which of these ways of expressing your faith would you like to grow, and why?

7. Where are you 'pressing on' in following Christ at the moment?

Wednesday 30 January

1. Why is it important to have a plan for reading the Bible? What plans or guides have you tried? Which ones would you recommend to others?

2. Do you find it encouraging or discouraging that it took Mary three years to read through the Bible? Why?

3. Do you read the longer Bible passage suggested with the meditations here each day? If so, how and why did you begin including them in your devotional time? If not, what might you gain by doing so?

4. Aside from the Bible, what book has had the greatest effect on your Christian life? How has it affected the way you live your faith?

5. What is your favourite Bible verse or story at the moment? Why might our favourites change over time?

6. What passages or stories from the Bible puzzle you? Why is trying to understand them important? When and why is it important to stop struggling to understand?

7. How has reading and discussing this meditation caused you to re-evaluate your approach to spiritual reading?

Wednesday 6 February

1. Whom do you consider to be your enemies personally or on a larger scale? Why are they enemies? Who do you think considers you an enemy, and why?

2. Recall a statement you have made about an enemy (and repeat it if you feel comfortable doing so). Does your statement show love for the enemy? Why or why not?

3. Jesus spoke about enemies more than once. What does this say to you about having and being enemies?

4. According to Exodus 23:4–5, we are not to ignore the problems of our enemies. What might this mean to you in everyday life? What if anything might you have to do differently to live in the spirit of these verses?

5. When have you been tempted to retaliate but restrained yourself from doing so? How were you able to do this? Why did you want or decide to hold back?

6. How can the Church model Christian ways of dealing with our enemies?

Wednesday 13 February

1. What are some strategies you have heard of or used to help you remember things? Which ones are most effective for you?

2. When have you forgotten a birthday, anniversary or other important occasion? What caused you finally to remember it? How did you feel and what did you do about forgetting?

3. What was the subject of the last sermon you heard? What scripture verses or story was/were used? At the time, did you think it was a good sermon? What action did you consider because of hearing the sermon?

4. Why do you remember or not remember sermons? Does God want us to remember what we hear in them? How might we help ourselves to remember what God says to us through preachers and other believers?

5. Deuteronomy 8:2 commands us to remember 'the way the Lord [our] God has led' us. Name three or four important events in your spiritual journey. Why are they important?

6. In what ways/by what means has God offered you hope in times of suffering? How have you experienced his presence with you in a time of suffering?

7. What have you learned from your times of suffering that has affected how you respond to others who are suffering?

8. How could being with others in their suffering help us to find peace?

Wednesday 20 February

1. Do you usually give up something for Lent? If so, how do you decide what to give up? If not, what do you think this practice does for others?

2. What have you learned about God and yourself through denying yourself something you enjoy? Why would God want us to deliberately avoid activities we enjoy?

3. What do you think of Laura's Lenten practice? Is it one that you might consider taking up? Why or why not?

4. Besides praying, what are some other positive practices we might take up for Lent?

5. Which possible Lenten practices mentioned in response to the last question would you be most likely to adopt and why?

6. How might taking up a positive practice for Lent help us to identify more closely with Jesus as we approach Easter?

7. What spiritual practices help you to feel closer to Christ?

8. Laura used an ordinary occurrence as a call to prayer. What event or feeling might you use as a call to prayer in the coming week? What would you pray for?

Wednesday 27 February

1. When has a stranger's small act of kindness made a difference in your life and in how you felt about yourself? Why did it make a difference for you?

2. Do you think you would have done what the woman mentioned here did? Why or why not?

3. What do you suppose caused the woman to speak to Charles? What might she have seen that caused her to reach out to him? What do you think the other people in the waiting room felt or thought when they witnessed the events Charles describes?

4. When did you last encounter an 'outsider'? What was the situation, and what did you do?

5. Think back to a time when you felt left out. What could someone have done in that situation to make you feel included and accepted?

6. What people 'of low position' do you encounter regularly? Do you make it a point to interact with them? Do you think God wants us to? How might we affirm such people's worth and dignity without seeming condescending?

7. Why should we push ourselves to perform acts of kindness that don't come naturally to us?

Wednesday 6 March

1. Did you move frequently while you were growing up? If so, what did that feel like? What were the positives and the negatives of that way of life? If you lived in the same place the whole time you were growing up, what were the positives and negatives?

2. Of all the places you have lived in your life, which place was your favourite, and why? Did you feel happiest in your favourite place? Why? Do our surroundings have an effect on how we feel? Why or why not?

3. Read Psalm 139:1–10 aloud. What are the positives and negatives of the psalmist's view of God? Do the words of the Psalm help you to feel God's presence with you now, at this moment? Will you remember them throughout the day? How will they affect you as you go about your daily tasks?

4. In what ways does your church home provide stability, comfort and security for you? If you are someone who has moved around a lot, have you found it difficult to find these things in a church community, where you are often a 'new' person? How have you dealt with this? How would you advise other people in the same situation?

5. The writer says that most of us face major life changes and the stresses that come with those changes. How has that been true in your life? What are your sources of strength during these challenging times? Have such changes made you stronger or not? If so, how has this happened?

6. Who do you know who is facing the stresses of moving? What can your church community do to help? How can you help? Can you think of practical ways in which your church can reach out to new people in your neighbourhood, perhaps by providing a meal, or childcare?

7. Do you feel, like the psalmist does, that you cannot flee from the presence of God? How does God's constant presence help you deal with the stresses of life? Do you feel reassured to know that he is with you constantly? If not, what would convince you that he is with you?

Wednesday 13 March

1. Have you ever watched a plant re-bloom when you thought it was dead? Describe how that experience happened for you. Has it made you change the way in which you look after your plants? How would you go about this?

2. The writer speaks poignantly about the struggles with her son. Have you had similar struggles in your family? Or do you know someone who has? Was there a transformation, as there was in this writer's family? What happened?

3. The Hebrews passage speaks about faith, and describes it in various ways. Read the passage and think about which description of faith best represents how you think of faith. Why do you think this? Are your feelings about faith based on long experience, or are they relatively new? What things have happened in your life to strengthen—or threaten—your faith?

4. Is there a family in your church community who is struggling with a situation like the one in this meditation? What kind of help can you provide? Can your congregation provide? Have you considered praying for, or with, the people concerned? Why or why not?

5. In what ways is the message of Hebrews 11:1 reflected in this story? How hard is it to put our faith in something we cannot see? Does it become easier with time and experience, when we can look back and see where our faith has helped us in the past? Can you describe a time when your faith helped you through a tough time?

Wednesday 20 March

1. When was the last time you attempted a home improvement project that didn't turn out well? What happened? When did you have a successful project? What happened? Do you approach such tasks differently now?

2. Do you, like the writer, often try to use the wrong life tools? Describe a time when that happened. Did you get hurt like this writer did? How did you resolve the situation? Did you learn anything to help you in another, similar dilemma? What was it?

3. What role do prayer and Bible study play in your decision-making? Do you have a discipline for these? If so, describe it. If not, ask a trusted friend to help you establish a discipline.

4. What role can your church community play in helping others use the tools of Bible study and prayer? What does your church offer in these areas? If it does not offer such things, could you help to establish a weekly Bible study and prayer meeting? Are there people you could ask to help? Will you contact them this week? Today?

5. What part of the Bible do you first go to when you need answers? Is it always the same part? Why? Have you tried other parts of the Bible when you need specific help? Do you use the 'Helps' section at the front of *The Upper Room*? Why or why not?

Wednesday 27 March

1. What is your view of tithing? What does your church say about it? Is tithing a regular part of your giving? If not, would you consider starting after reading this meditation?

2. Do you agree with the writer's statement: 'the more we give away, the more we get back'? When have you seen this happen? To you personally? How did it make you feel? Did it change your attitude to tithing, or other giving? In what way?

3. What other ways (besides money) can what is given away be given back? Are you aware of using your God-given gifts in a way that gives them back to him? How do you go about this? How might you do this in the future?

4. What mission projects could your church be involved with? How could your tithes be used for good in the community? Does your church set aside specific sums of money to help people in the community who are struggling? If it does not, is this a way the church could witness to the community?

5. In the 2 Corinthians passage (9:6–15), Paul is giving thanks to the Corinthian church members for their generosity. If Paul were writing about your church today, for what activities would he be expressing gratitude? Can these activities be extended? Are there talents in your church community that are under-used? How can they be developed into new activities?

Wednesday 3 April

1. Have you ever compared the biblical accounts of the resurrection? After reading the meditation, would you? How are they different? Which account tells you the most? Why? From which account did you learn something new? What is it, and how does it add to your understanding?

2. What do you think about the resurrection? Have your views changed during your Christian life? How? Is the resurrection the most important aspect of your Christian belief? Why or why not? If it is not, what is?

3. How much does the resurrection feature in your Bible study or in discussions with other Christians? How does your understanding differ from that of other people? In what ways? Do you find it helpful to hear others' opinions, or not? How would it affect your own faith in what you believe to hear radically different opinions?

4. Do you meet or worship with Christians from other denominations? Why or why not? What can we learn from each other? Would it promote better understanding among your church community to have fellowship with other denominations? Do you think the differences between the denominations are good or bad? Why do you think the way you do?

5. Does the resurrection feature in your conversations with non-Christians? How would you describe it to someone who knows nothing about it? Would it be obvious to that person that you feel it is an important part of your Christian faith? Why?

Wednesday 10 April

1. Have you ever tried using a verse of scripture as a motto for the day, as Ruth describes? Why would this be a good habit to adopt? How would it change your day to practise using a Scripture verse through it? Will you try it from today or tomorrow? If not, why would you not try it?

2. How easy is it to talk about people behind their backs? Do you? How does it make you feel? Do you think people talk about you in a similar way? Do you think criticising someone to a third party is ever justified? Why do you think it is, or is not?

3. Do you hear criticism of others in your church community? If so, why do you think this happens in a place where love and acceptance should be paramount? What sort of message would this give out to a new Christian who joins your church? What can you do to address the problem?

4. Have you ever hurt someone by what you have said about them? Have you ever been hurt in the same way? How did it make you feel? How have you dealt with the person you hurt, or hurt you? How has it affected your relationship in each case? Would the way you feel stop you from hurting someone again?

5. Do you ask God to 'watch over the door of [your] lips'? How important is it to do so? Why? In your dealings with others, do you try to think before you speak? Will you do so from now on? How easy or hard will that be for you? How will you try and make sure you succeed?

Wednesday 17 April

1. How important is it to remember and pass on words of scripture to the next generation, as we read in the quotation from Deuteronomy? In talking to your children, grandchildren, or children at school or Sunday school, how much are you aware of doing this? What is the best way to go about it?

2. How can we learn from children? Does your church community take time to listen to the children in their midst? Do they have a voice in what goes on in church worship programmes, in teaching and other activities? How important do you think this is? What reasons do you give for your response?

3. Do we as adults complicate our faith unnecessarily? Why do we do this? Is it better to approach our faith as a child does, talking simply to God, listening to stories about him, and praying and caring for others in the way that a child would? Or is that too simplistic? How would it work for you?

4. Are we preoccupied too much with everything we have to do, so that our faith is not uppermost in our mind? Do we try to juggle too many things? How can we simplify our lives so that God is first with us? If we tried to do that, would it also simplify the rest of life, and would it be easier to do what has to be done?

5. How do you think other people regard us: as people of a strong but simple faith (like a child) or as someone who makes life unnecessarily complicated (like many adults)? How would you prefer to be remembered? What things can you change about yourself and the way you live so that your faith is like a child's instead?

Wednesday 24 April

1. Do you identify with the comments about witness in this meditation? Why or why not? How many times have you spoken about your own relationship with Christ to another person? What might prompt you to do so? What might prevent you from doing so?

2. Is there a specific activity within your church aimed at witnessing in your community? What form does it take? Is it important that people in the community know why we are Christians? Is it a requirement of our faith that we speak to people in this organised way? What would encourage you to do so? What might discourage you?

3. How important is it to offer 'deeds' as a Christian witness, as well as 'words'? Which is more important? Can visiting the sick and the lonely be a witness as much as talking to people about our faith? Should the second arise from the first, or should it be the other way around? Which are you more comfortable with? Why?

4. What is the most important thing about your faith that you would want to share with another person? How would you go about it? Would you offer it as a solution to someone's problems? Should you wait until they ask you about it, or would you be happy to initiate a conversation and see where it led? Would you feel guided by God to say the right thing? How would you know?

5. How would people you meet know that you are a Christian? Do others know of the 'courage and strength and love Christ brings to [your] life'? Are you challenged by this idea? If so, how could you go about making it apparent that Christ is important to you? Would you want to do so? Why or why not?

When You Pray

Daily Bible reflections for Lent and Easter on the Lord's Prayer

Joanna Collicutt

In these Bible readings for Lent and Easter, Joanna Collicutt shows how growing as a Christian is rooted in the prayer Jesus gave us. As we pray the Lord's Prayer, we express our relationship with God, absorb gospel values and are also motivated to live them out. As we pray to the Father, in union with the Son, through the power of the Spirit, so we begin to take on the character of Christ. The Holy Week readings encourage us to pause, watch and wait at this special season; commentary is kept to a minimum and we spend time reflecting, in the light of the Lord's Prayer, on Luke's description of Christ's passion and resurrection.

When You Pray includes group study matrial. Free video resources to support this book for Lent reading groups and personal study are also available at www.youtube.com/brfonline

ISBN 978 0 85746 089 9   £7.99
To order a copy of this book, please turn to the order form on page 159.

Also available for Kindle.

Servant Ministry

A portrait of Christ and a pattern for his followers

Tony Horsfall

Servanthood is something to which all believers are called, not just those in full-time ministry. This means that understanding what servanthood means is vital for the health and well-being of local churches. Every member needs to appreciate their role as a servant of God. At the same time, the principles of servant-leadership provide an essential framework for those called specifically to the work of the church, whether at home or overseas.

Servant Ministry offers a practical exposition of the first 'Servant Song' in Isaiah (42:1–9). Writing from many years of Christian teaching and mentoring, Tony Horsfall applies insights drawn from the Isaiah passage to topics such as the motivation for service and the call to serve; valid expressions of servanthood and the link between evangelism and social action; character formation and what it means to be a servant; how to keep going over the long haul in the harsh realities of ministry; the importance of listening to God on a daily basis and also over a whole lifetime.

ISBN 978 0 85746 088 2 £7.99
To order a copy of this book, please turn to the order form on page 159.

Also available for Kindle.

Spiritual Care of Dying and Bereaved People

Penelope Wilcock

This book is about life, not death. When we are with people approaching death, we feel a sense of awe, the solemnity of a great and sacred moment approaching. To accompany other people, along with their loved ones, up to the gate of death, is to enter holy ground; to stand in an awesome place where the wind of the Spirit blows, to encounter peace and grief, insight, intimacy and pain on a level not found in ordinary living.

An updated and expanded edition of a classic book, *Spiritual Care of Dying and Bereaved People* is a fresh, original and honest look at death and bereavement, including the author's personal experiences. Most of us don't realise how much we have to offer to those who are dying or bereaved. This book encourages readers to grow in confidence as companions, looking honestly at the questions people ask and offering a reflection on the kind of God those questions reveal. This new edition also includes a practical section on how to plan a funeral.

ISBN 978 1 84101 115 5   £9.99

To order a copy of this book, please turn to the order form on page 159.

Everything I Know about God, I've Learned from Being a Parent

Veronica Zundel

The Bible tells us that God is 'the Father, from whom every family in heaven and on earth takes its name' (Ephesians 3:15). If earthly families gain their nature from God's parenthood, what might our experience of family tell us about the nature of God? That is the question on which this book focuses.

Veronica Zundel roots her reflections in her journey into and through parenthood, a hard journey that led through infertility, late motherhood and then learning to parent a child with special needs. What she learned along the way—about love and sacrifice, faithfulness and forgiveness—had a profound impact on her understanding of what God feels about us, his most beloved children.

ISBN 978 1 84101 416 6 £6.99
To order a copy of this book, please turn to the order form on page 159.

Also available for Kindle.

Bible Reading Resources Pack

Thank you for reading BRF Bible reading notes. BRF has been producing a variety of Bible reading notes for over 90 years, helping people all over the UK and the world connect with the Bible on a personal level every day.

Could you help us find other people who would enjoy our notes?

We produce a Bible Reading Resource Pack for church groups to use to encourage regular Bible reading.

This FREE pack contains:

- Samples of all BRF Bible reading notes.
- Our Resources for Personal Bible Reading catalogue, providing all you need to know about our Bible reading notes.
- A ready-to-use church magazine feature about BRF notes.
- Ready-made sermon and all-age service ideas to help your church into the Bible (ideal for Bible Sunday events).
- And much more!

How to order your FREE pack:

- Visit: www.biblereadingnotes.org.uk/request-a-bible-reading-resources-pack/
- Telephone: 01865 319700
- Post: Complete the form below and post to: Bible Reading Resource Pack, BRF, 15 The Chambers, Vineyard, Abingdon, OX14 3FE

Name..

Address ....

....Postcode...

Telephone ....

Email..

Please send me...................................Bible Reading Resources Pack(s).

This pack is produced free of charge for all UK addresses but, if you wish to offer a donation towards our costs, this would be appreciated. If you require a pack to be sent outside of the UK, please contact us for details of postage and packing charges. Tel: +44 1865 319700. Thank you.

BRF is a Registered Charity

Subscriptions

The Upper Room is published in January, May and September.

Individual subscriptions

The subscription rate for orders for 4 or fewer copies includes postage and packing: THE UPPER ROOM annual individual subscription £14.10

Church subscriptions

Orders for 5 copies or more, sent to ONE address, are post free:
THE UPPER ROOM annual church subscription £11.10

Please do not send payment with order for a church subscription. We will send an invoice with your first order.

Please note that the annual billing period for church subscriptions runs from 1 May to 30 April.

Copies of the notes may also be obtained from Christian bookshops.

Single copies of *The Upper Room* will cost £3.70. Prices valid until 30 April 2014.

Giant print version

The Upper Room is available in giant print for the visually impaired, from:

Torch Trust for the Blind
Torch House
Torch Way,
Northampton Road
Market Harborough
LE16 9HL

Tel: 01858 438260
www.torchtrust.org

Individual Subscriptions

☐ I would like to take out a subscription myself (complete your name and address details only once)

☐ I would like to give a gift subscription (please complete both name and address sections below)

Your name...

Your address...

....Postcode.......................................

Your telephone number..

Gift subscription name..

Gift subscription address..

....Postcode.......................................

Gift message (20 words max)...

....

Please send *The Upper Room* beginning with the May 2013 / September 2013 / January 2014 issue: (delete as applicable)

THE UPPER ROOM ☐ £14.10

Please complete the payment details below and send, with appropriate payment, to: BRF, 15 The Chambers, Vineyard, Abingdon OX14 3FE

Total enclosed £ .... (cheques should be made payable to 'BRF')

Payment by ☐ cheque ☐ postal order ☐ Visa ☐ Mastercard ☐ Switch

Card no:																					

Expires: ☐☐☐☐   Security code: ☐☐☐

Issue no (Switch): ☐☐☐☐

Signature (essential if paying by credit/Switch card) ....

☐ Please do not send me further information about BRF publications

☐ Please send me a Bible reading resources pack to encourage Bible reading in my church

BRF is a Registered Charity

Church Subscriptions

☐ Please send me ... copies of *The Upper Room* May 2013 / September 2013 / January 2014 issue (delete as applicable)

Name...

Address ....

....Postcode..

Telephone ....

Email...

Please send this completed form to:
BRF, 15 The Chambers, Vineyard, Abingdon OX14 3FE

Please do not send payment with this order. We will send an invoice with your first order.

Christian bookshops: All good Christian bookshops stock BRF publications. For your nearest stockist, please contact BRF.

Telephone: The BRF office is open between 09.15 and 17.30. To place your order, telephone 01865 319700; fax 01865 319701.

Web: Visit www.brf.org.uk

☐ Please send me a Bible reading resources pack to encourage Bible reading in my church

BRF is a Registered Charity

ORDERFORM

REF	TITLE	PRICE	QTY	TOTAL
089 9	When You Pray	£7.99		
088 2	Servant Ministry	£7.99		
115 5	Spiritual Care Dying/Bereaved People	£9.99		
416 6	Everything I Know about God…	£6.99		

POSTAGE AND PACKING CHARGES				
Order value	UK	Europe	Surface	Air Mail
£7.00 & under	£1.25	£3.00	£3.50	£5.50
£7.01–£30.00	£2.25	£5.50	£6.50	£10.00
Over £30.00	FREE	prices on request		

Postage and packing	
Donation	
TOTAL	

Name _____ Account Number _____

Address _____

_____ Postcode _____

Telephone Number_____

Email _____

Payment by: ❑ Cheque ❑ Mastercard ❑ Visa ❑ Postal Order ❑ Maestro

Card no ❑❑❑❑ ❑❑❑❑ ❑❑❑❑ ❑❑❑❑ ❑❑❑

Valid from ❑❑❑❑ Expires ❑❑❑❑ Issue no. ❑❑❑

Security code* ❑❑❑ *Last 3 digits on the reverse of the card.
ESSENTIAL IN ORDER TO PROCESS YOUR ORDER Shaded boxes for Maestro use only

Signature _____ Date _____

All orders must be accompanied by the appropriate payment.

Please send your completed order form to:
BRF, 15 The Chambers, Vineyard, Abingdon OX14 3FE
Tel. 01865 319700 / Fax. 01865 319701 Email: enquiries@brf.org.uk

❑ Please send me further information about BRF publications.

Available from your local Christian bookshop.   BRF is a Registered Charity

About
brf:

BRF is a registered charity and also a limited company, and has been in existence since 1922. Through all that we do—producing resources, providing training, working face-to-face with adults and children, and via the web—we work to resource individuals and church communities in their Christian discipleship through the Bible, prayer and worship.

Our Barnabas children's team works with primary schools and churches to help children under 11, and the adults who work with them, to explore Christianity creatively and to bring the Bible alive.

To find out more about BRF and its core activities and ministries, visit:

www.brf.org.uk
www.brfonline.org.uk
www.biblereadingnotes.org.uk
www.barnabasinschools.org.uk
www.barnabasinchurches.org.uk
www.faithinhomes.org.uk
www.messychurch.org.uk
www.foundations21.net

If you have any questions about BRF
and our work, please email us at

enquiries@brf.org.uk